PLAY ON SHAKESPEARE

Love's Labour's Lost

PLAY ON SHAKESPEARE

All's Well That Ends Well	Virginia Grise
Antony and Cleopatra	Christopher Chen
As You Like It	David Ivers
The Comedy of Errors	Christina Anderson
Coriolanus	Sean San José
Cymbeline	Andrea Thome
Edward III	Octavio Solis
Hamlet	Lisa Peterson
Henry IV	Yvette Nolan
Henry V	Lloyd Suh
Henry VI	Douglas P. Langworthy
Henry VIII	Caridad Svich
Julius Caesar	Shishir Kurup
King John	Brighde Mullins
King Lear	Marcus Gardley
Love's Labour's Lost	Josh Wilder
Macbeth	Migdalia Cruz
Measure for Measure	Aditi Brennan Kapil
The Merchant of Venice	Elise Thoron
The Merry Wives of Windsor	Dipika Guha
A Midsummer Night's Dream	Jeffrey Whitty
Much Ado About Nothing	Ranjit Bolt
Othello	Mfoniso Udofia
Pericles	Ellen McLaughlin
Richard II	Naomi Iizuka
Richard III	Migdalia Cruz
Romeo and Juliet	Hansol Jung
The Taming of the Shrew	Amy Freed
The Tempest	Kenneth Cavander
Timon of Athens	Kenneth Cavander
Titus Andronicus	Amy Freed
Troilus and Cressida	Lillian Groag
Twelfth Night	Alison Carey
The Two Gentlemen of Verona	Amelia Roper
The Two Noble Kinsmen	Tim Slover
The Winter's Tale	Tracy Young

Love's Labour's Lost

by
William Shakespeare

Modern verse translation by
Josh Wilder

Dramaturgy by
Davina Moss

Arizona State University
Tempe, Arizona
2024

———

*Publication of Play On Shakespeare is assisted by
generous support from the Hitz Foundation.
For more information, please visit* www.playonshakespeare.org

———

Published by ACMRS Press
Arizona Center for Medieval and Renaissance Studies,
Arizona State University, Tempe, Arizona
www.acmrspress.com

Library of Congress Cataloging-in-Publication Data
Names: Wilder, Josh, 1990- author. | Moss, Davina, contributor. |
    Shakespeare, William, 1564-1616. Love's labour's lost.
Title: Love's labour's lost / by William Shakespeare ; modern verse
    translation by Josh Wilder ; dramaturgy by Davina Moss.
Description: Tempe, Arizona : ACMRS Press, 2024. | Series: Play on
    Shakespeare | Summary: "A wacky comedy of disguise and mischief,
    following the King of Navarre and his companions as they attempt to
    swear off the company of women in updated language that brings out
    the play's romp and sass for a contemporary audience"-- Provided by
    publisher.
Identifiers: LCCN 2023044987 (print) | LCCN 2023044988 (ebook) |
    ISBN 9780866988230 (paperback) | ISBN 9780866988247 (ebook)
Subjects: LCSH: Courts and courtiers--Drama. | Princesses--Drama. |
    Navarre (Kingdom)--Drama. | LCGFT: Comedy plays. | Adaptations.
Classification: LCC PR2878.L6 W55 2024 (print) | LCC PR2878.L6
    (ebook) | DDC 812/.6--dc23/eng/20231017
LC record available at https://lccn.loc.gov/2023044987
LC ebook record available at https://lccn.loc.gov/2023044988

Printed in the United States of America

We wish to acknowledge our gratitude
for the extraordinary generosity of the
Hitz Foundation

∽

Special thanks to the Play On Shakespeare staff
Lue Douthit, President and Co-Founder
Taylor Bailey, Producing Director
Cheryl Rizzo, Business Director
Artie Calvert, Finance Director

∽

Originally commissioned by the
Oregon Shakespeare Festival
Bill Rauch, Artistic Director
Cynthia Rider, Executive Director

PLAY ON SHAKESPEARE

In 2015, the Oregon Shakespeare Festival announced a new commissioning program. It was called "Play on!: 36 playwrights translate Shakespeare." It elicited a flurry of reactions. For some people this went too far: "You can't touch the language!" For others, it didn't go far enough: "Why not new adaptations?" I figured we would be on the right path if we hit the sweet spot in the middle.

Some of the reaction was due not only to the scale of the project, but its suddenness: 36 playwrights, along with 38 dramaturgs, had been commissioned and assigned to translate 39 plays, and they were already hard at work on the assignment. It also came fully funded by the Hitz Foundation with the shocking sticker price of $3.7 million.

I think most of the negative reaction, however, had to do with the use of the word "translate." It's been difficult to define precisely. It turns out that there is no word for the kind of subtle and rigorous examination of language that we are asking for. We don't mean "word for word," which is what most people think of when they hear the word translate. We don't mean "paraphrase," either.

The project didn't begin with 39 commissions. Linguist John McWhorter's musings about translating Shakespeare is what sparked this project. First published in his 1998 book *Word on the Street* and reprinted in 2010 in *American Theatre* magazine, he notes that the "irony today is that the Russians, the French, and other people in foreign countries possess Shakespeare to a much greater extent than we do, for the simple reason that they get to enjoy Shakespeare in the language they speak."

This intrigued Dave Hitz, a long-time patron of the Oregon Shakespeare Festival, and he offered to support a project that looked at Shakespeare's plays through the lens of the English we speak today. How much has the English language changed since Shakespeare? Is it possible that there are conventions in the early modern English of Shakespeare that don't translate to us today, especially in the moment of hearing it spoken out loud as one does in the theater?

How might we "carry forward" the successful communication between actor and audience that took place 400 years ago? "Carry forward," by the way, is what we mean by "translate." It is the fourth definition of *translate* in the Oxford English Dictionary.

As director of literary development and dramaturgy at the Oregon Shakespeare Festival, I was given the daunting task of figuring out how to administer the project. I began with Kenneth Cavander, who translates ancient Greek tragedies into English. I figured that someone who does that kind of work would lend an air of seriousness to the project. I asked him how might he go about translating from the source language of early modern English into the target language of contemporary modern English?

He looked at different kinds of speech: rhetorical and poetical, soliloquies and crowd scenes, and the puns in comedies. What emerged from his tinkering became a template for the translation commission. These weren't rules exactly, but instructions that every writer was given.

First, do no harm. There is plenty of the language that doesn't need translating. And there is some that does. Every playwright had different criteria for assessing what to change.

Second, go line-by-line. No editing, no cutting, no "fixing." I want the whole play translated. We often cut the gnarly bits in

Shakespeare for performance. What might we make of those bits if we understood them in the moment of hearing them? Might we be less compelled to cut?

Third, all other variables stay the same: the time period, the story, the characters, their motivations, and their thoughts. We designed the experiment to examine the language.

Fourth, and most important, the language must follow the same kind of rigor and pressure as the original, which means honoring the meter, rhyme, rhetoric, image, metaphor, character, action, and theme. Shakespeare's astonishingly compressed language must be respected. Trickiest of all: making sure to work within the structure of the iambic pentameter.

We also didn't know which of Shakespeare's plays might benefit from this kind of investigation: the early comedies, the late tragedies, the highly poetic plays. So we asked three translators who translate plays from other languages into English to examine a Shakespeare play from each genre outlined in the *First Folio*: Kenneth took on *Timon of Athens,* a tragedy; Douglas Langworthy worked on the *Henry the Sixth* history plays, and Ranjit Bolt tried his hand at the comedy *Much Ado about Nothing.*

Kenneth's *Timon* received a production at the Alabama Shakespeare in 2014 and it was on the plane ride home that I thought about expanding the project to include 39 plays. And I wanted to do them all at once. The idea was to capture a snapshot of contemporary modern English. I couldn't oversee that many commissions, and when Ken Hitz (Dave's brother and president of the Hitz Foundation) suggested that we add a dramaturg to each play, the plan suddenly unfolded in front of me. The next day, I made a simple, but extensive, proposal to Dave on how to commission and develop 39 translations in three years. He responded immediately with "Yes."

My initial thought was to only commission translators who translate plays. But I realized that "carry forward" has other meanings. There was a playwright in the middle of the conversation 400 years ago. What would it mean to carry *that* forward?

For one thing, it would mean that we wanted to examine the texts through the lens of performance. I am interested in learning how a dramatist makes sense of the play. Basically, we asked the writers to create performable companion pieces.

I wanted to tease out what we mean by contemporary modern English, and so we created a matrix of writers who embodied many different lived experiences: age, ethnicity, gender-identity, experience with translations, geography, English as a second language, knowledge of Shakespeare, etc.

What the playwrights had in common was a deep love of language and a curiosity about the assignment. Not everyone was on board with the idea and I was eager to see how the experiment would be for them. They also pledged to finish the commission within three years.

To celebrate the completion of the translations, we produced a festival in June 2019 in partnership with The Classic Stage Company in New York to hear all 39 of them. Four hundred years ago I think we went to *hear* a play; today we often go to *see* a play. In the staged reading format of the Festival, we heard these plays as if for the first time. The blend of Shakespeare with another writer was seamless and jarring at the same time. Countless actors and audience members told us that the plays were understandable in ways they had never been before.

Now it's time to share the work. We were thrilled when Ayanna Thompson and her colleagues at the Arizona Center for Medieval and Renaissance Studies offered to publish the translations for us.

I ask that you think of these as marking a moment in time.

The editions published in this series are based on the scripts that were used in the Play on! Festival in 2019. For the purpose of the readings, there were cuts allowed and these scripts represent those reading drafts.

The original commission tasked the playwrights and dramaturg to translate the whole play. The requirement of the commission was for two drafts which is enough to put the ball in play. The real fun with these texts is when there are actors, a director, a dramaturg, and the playwright wrestling with them together in a rehearsal room.

The success of a project of this scale depends on the collaboration and contributions of many people. The playwrights and dramaturgs took the assignment seriously and earnestly and were humble and gracious throughout the development of the translations. Sally Cade Holmes and Holmes Productions, our producer since the beginning, provided a steady and calm influence.

We have worked with more than 1,200 artists in the development of these works. We have partnered with more than three dozen theaters and schools. Numerous readings and more than a dozen productions of these translations have been heard and seen in the United States as well as Canada, England, and the Czech Republic.

There is a saying in the theater that 80% of the director's job is taken care of when the production is cast well. Such was my luck when I hired Taylor Bailey, who has overseen every reading and workshop, and was the producer of the Festival in New York. Katie Kennedy has gathered all the essays, and we have been supported by the rest of the Play on Shakespeare team: Kamilah Long, Summer Martin, and Amrita Ramanan.

All of this has come to be because Bill Rauch, then artistic director of the Oregon Shakespeare Festival, said yes when Dave

Hitz pitched the idea to him in 2011. Actually he said, "Hmm, interesting," which I translated to "yes." I am dearly indebted to that 'yes.'

My gratitude to Dave, Ken, and the Hitz Foundation can never be fully expressed. Their generosity, patience, and unwavering belief in what we are doing has given us the confidence to follow the advice of Samuel Beckett: "Ever tried. Ever failed. No matter. Try again. Fail again. Fail better."

Play on!

Dr. Lue Douthit
CEO/Creative Director at Play on Shakespeare
October 2020

Love's Labour's Lost

by Josh Wilder

The Courage to Play

My earliest memory of understanding Shakespeare was at the Queen Memorial Library on 22nd and Federal Street in South Philadelphia. It was the early 2000s and the library had become a safe haven for me, I spent plenty of hours of cultivating my imagination — there was a point though that I wanted to challenge my reading level — Ms. Sarah the librarian pointed to the shelf where they were selling old books. All Shakespeare. Me and my catholic school education sat down with a ruler, a red pen, and a dictionary and powered though *Titus Andronicus*. I understood bloody, gory, eat your brains Shakespeare — I loved it, but the comprehension headaches lingered. It wasn't later until I got to high school where I would read Shakespeare standing up.

This time it was *Julius Caesar*, I'm a 15-year-old theater major sitting in English class and a Vietnam vet named Mr. Brown was the substitute for the semester. Which one of the drama majors wants to read this monologue from *Julius Caesar*? My hand shot up and I eagerly went to the front of the class to perform the famous Brutus speech. I never struggled to read so much, I stuttered, tripped over my words, I covered it up with my "Shakespeare voice." "STOP SOUNDING BRITISH, AIN'T YOU PHILLY?!" "but it's Shakespeare" "No, no, no! Let me show you." Mr. Brown directed me to my seat and he transformed the room into the theater "Friends, Romans, Countrymen lend me your ears." I've never had a more impactful substitute, he spoke the speech as if he was on the block — the turned poetry into vernacular, I wanted to be a Shakespearean actor like him. After class I asked him, how did he do it. I'm a veteran, I understand this play and this monologue deeply. His advice to me was find a piece that spoke to me — naturally he gave me *Othello*. I studied and studied and knew it like I knew my favorite book. I used the Act 4 monologue for all my auditions for conservatory mimicking the performance of my substitute teacher.

Fast forward to 2010, I'm second year acting student at Carnegie Mellon and it's my hardest year ever. We were to study Shakespeare all year, the first semester in speech class, the second in scene study. I distinctly remember being in acting class, struggling with the balcony scene, my professor Tony Mckay — he was an acting teacher with nerves of steel. Stoic, direct, yet warm — I was working on my dream role and for the life of me, I couldn't make the poetry that I memorized in my head sink into my body. Do it this way! Do it that way! Try this! Use the words! I cursed him out in frustration and embarrassment. He cursed me out right back! Do the scene again, and this time don't forget you're a young boy in love! You're not at a poetry recital. Stop letting the poetry fool you! Sometimes you gotta get cursed out to get the point. I finally got the words in my body when it came to do the scene weeks later. I felt it. All of it, but I still didn't understand it. What was wrong with me? Later that year in the spring, I played the Wall in *Midsummer* — I understood everything and had a ton of fun. The director who happened to be my speech teacher that gave me a D in Shakespeare was elated by my progress. I went further in my head, why am I better as the blue collar mechanical than the courtly lover Romeo? Is it because, is it because, is it because? I hung up my Shakespeare hat at the tender age of 20, I was done with the Bard. I quit acting in my head and set my focus on writing plays. I was gonna tell my own stories and be my own Shakespeare, to test my own mettle I sent my first play to the Oregon Shakespeare Festival.

Three years later: Enter Lue Douthit, on a mission and pursued by a bear. When Lue approached me about Play On! I was nervous, I was just about to begin my time at Yale School of Drama; my playwriting career was just beginning; and I knew that once I said yes to this project there would be proverbial target on my back especially by the Shakespearean scholars and purists. At the same time, I was honored to join this group of rebel playwrights that I greatly admired. I was going to grad school anyway, why not? Maybe I'll come out as a better writer on the other side. Unknowingly my first year at YSD would be the most critical to this process. With all my trepidations about going back to school, and the battle scars I had from undergrad I prepared for an uphill climb of imposter syndrome and institutional racism in hopes of some artistic transformation. Surprisingly, my first day of orientation I discovered that I was a part of a new beginning at YSD. Surrounded by who I hoped to be lifelong colleagues, I was ensured on day one that I had a place at the table.

What did I want to accomplish the most with this translation? I wanted to find my way into to text so I can be in conversation with the story of *Love's Labour's Lost*; maintain the musicality of the play; bring out the romp and sass of being a hormonal teenager within the academy; and solidify Rosaline as a Black character in this world. Before I could attempt to accomplish any of the tasks ahead, I first had to study. Here's what I learned: Shakespeare wrote for the working class, most of us know this section of audience as the groundlings, the peanut gallery, or the cheap seats. What about these groundlings are so special? They make or break the play. I could only imagine being in a new play process where the audience could easily revolt and shut down the stage if they were bored. The groundlings were the temperature check of the plays story and structure, they indeed were the real directors of new play development. The groundlings were also the everyday people who made England run — they were the working class. But what about the other tiers in the audience? The people of the court? Indeed he catered to them too, and he made fun of them. What pressure to be under as a new playwright during Shakespeare's times.

Now it was my time to translate this centuries old text into something familiar. Something that all ears can understand. Every time I sat down to examine *Love's Labour's Lost* my understanding of the word, the text, and the characters got deeper and deeper. My takeaway? This is a story about young people who are learning how to be adults until they are forced to. That became the anchor for my translation.

I didn't want my voice to be the loudest in the text. My goal was to be an invisible influence, to work with what was already there without taking the reader out of their sphere. I didn't want to rewrite the play, I wanted to open the play up, so the actors can play on. So I cut the Latin, streamlined Berowne's speeches, and amped up the raunchy rhetoric just a bit. I couldn't do this all alone. My dramaturg Davina Moss and I spent hours on this task, traveling the world in order to gauge the play's temperature on young actors. I distinctly remember one summer at Tofte Lake, spending days on Berowne's speeches; or in London in a tiny flat debating the definition of the word "fair" with regards to Rosaline. Cross cultural collaboration truly was the key to making this translation a success.

When we got the opportunity to workshop the play in New York, everything came together. With director Nelson Eusebio at the helm, a deja vu was happening. Another veteran guiding me through the text, making it clearer for me and the actors, challenging the words I was using, but most importantly getting to the bare bones of what was being communicated. It takes a village to raise a play, and it takes an army to modernize a classic. My hope when you read this translation is that you the reader won't have any comprehension anxiety, that you will find the humor, the love, and the tension of these teenagers in this world. Thank you Lue, and Play On! for trusting my voice and my perspective on this ancient new play.

CHARACTERS IN THE PLAY

(in order of speaking)

KING FERDINAND, King of Navarre
LORD LONGAVILLE, King's attendant
LORD DUMAINE, King's attendant
LORD BEROWNE, King's attendant
DULL, a constable
COSTARD, a clown
DON ADRIANO de ARMADO, a fantastical Spaniard
MOTH, Armado's page
JAQUENETTA, a country wench
BOYET, a lord and the Princess's attendant
PRINCESS OF FRANCE
LADY MARIA, the Princess's attendant
LADY KATHERINE, the Princess's attendant
LADY ROSALINE, the Princess's attendant
FORESTER
SIR NATHANIEL, a curate
HOLOFERNES, a pedant
MONSIEUR MARCADÉ, a messenger
Other Lords, Attendants, and Musicians

ACT 1 ◆ SCENE 1

Enter King Ferdinand and his Lords Berowne,
Longaville, and Dumaine

KING

Let fame, that all chase after in their lives,
Be etched upon our everlasting tombs,
And then grace us in the disgrace of death;
When, in spite of greedy devouring time,
The endeavour of this present breath may buy   5
That honour which shall dull the grave's keen edge,
And make us gods for all eternity.
Therefore, brave conquerors — for so you are,
That war against your proclivities
And the huge army of the world's sweet cravings —   10
This fresh decree shall strongly stand in force.
Navarre shall be a wonder of the world,
Our court shall be a great academy
That champions a new morality.
Berowne, Dumaine, and Longaville, you three,   15
My fellow-scholars, have sworn a three-year term
To live with me, and to keep these bylaws
That are recorded in this contract here.
You've made your oath, and now sign your names here,
That your own hand may strike your honour down   20
If you violate the smallest clause.
If you are armed to do as you swear to do,
Honour your deep oath, and keep it too.

LONGAVILLE

Why not? it's only a three years' fast.

1

The mind will flourish while the body moulds. 25
Fat bellies have no brains, and tasty bits
Make rich the ribs, but bankrupt quite the wits.

Longaville signs

DUMAINE

My loving king, I stand here full of shame.
The basest, most lascivious parts of life
God gives to the promiscuous ones. 30
Of love, of wealth, of fame, I starve and die,
With all these living in philosophy.

Dumaine signs

BEROWNE

I concur with all that has been said.
Dear king, you know I have already sworn,
That is, to "live and study here three years." 35
But let's discuss these observances here:
To not see a woman in three whole years,
Which I desperately hope is not God's truth;
And to not eat one day out of the week,
Though we're allowed but one meal a day, 40
I hope that's not what's in this charter, hey?
And then to sleep but three hours a night,
And behave as if we are not tired at all.
Sir, I'm accustomed to sleeping all night
And most times take a slumber in the day, 45
Which I hope is not a rule that will stay.
Oof, these are wasteful tasks, too hard to keep:
Not to see ladies, study, fast, not sleep.

KING

You gave me your word to abstain from these.

BEROWNE

Let me say no, my king, and if you please. 50

I only swore to study with your grace
And stay here in your court for three years' space.

LONGAVILLE

You swore to that, Berowne, and to the rest.

BEROWNE

I am deciding still, I swore in jest.
The point of this study, tell me the rest.   55

KING

Why, to know the things we don't yet know.

BEROWNE

Things hid and barred, you mean, from common sense?

KING

Ha, that is study's god-like recompense.

BEROWNE

Alright then, I will swear to study so,
To know the things I am forbid to know: 60
And so, to study when I'd rather eat,
Since where I would feast I am now "forbid"
Or study where to meet some mistress fine,
When mistresses from common sense are hid.
Or, having sworn too hard an oath to keep,   65
Study to break it, and not break my sleep.
If study's gain be this then God, I swear
That study knows what study does not show.
Swear me to this, and I will not say no.

KING

Are these the holes that stop pure study's flight   70
And trick our common sense to vain delight?

BEROWNE

Why, all delights are vain, but that most vain
Which, with all pleasures, does inherit pain:
As painfully to spread open a book

To seek the light of truth, while truth the while   75
Does falsely blind the eyesight of his look.
Light seeking light makes light of the aroused;
Let's search and find where light lies in the prowl,
Your light grows dark by shielding your "man's-eye."
Study me how to please that eye indeed   80
By fixing it upon a lady's eye,
Who dazzling so, that eye shall be his lead,
And give him light that it was blinded by.
Studying is like staring at the sun,
You hurt your eyes with the prolonged looks;   85
Blinded by words, they don't learn anything
Apart from what they learn from others' books.
These men, the academy's leading lights,
That give a name to every shining star,
Are no more different in stature and might   90
Than blokes that shuffle and know what they are.
Knowing all's just a mere pursuit of fame,
And every man around can give a name.

KING

How well he's read, to reason against reading.

DUMAINE

Proceeded well, to stop all good proceeding.   95

LONGAVILLE

He weeds the corn, and still lets grow the weeding.

BEROWNE

The spring is near when horny geese are breeding.

DUMAINE

How follows that?

BEROWNE

Fit in his place and time.

4

DUMAINE

In reason nothing. 100

BEROWNE

Something then in rhyme.

KING

Berowne is like that spiteful old Jack Frost,

That bites the first-born infants of the spring.

BEROWNE

Well, say I am. Why should proud summer boast

Before the birds have any cause to sing? 105

Why should I be happy when things go awry?

At Christmas I do not desire a rose

Or wish a snow in May's flowery shows,

But prefer each thing that in season grows.

So you, to study now it is too late, 110

Come on, it's spring: unlock the lover's gate.

KING

Well, take your leave. Go home, Berowne: you're through.

BEROWNE

No, my good lord, I have sworn to stay with you.

And sorry now for speaking out of turn,

I seem to have forgotten my place here, 115

I'm confident I'll keep what I have sworn

And keep my promises for all three year.

Give me the paper, let me read the same,

And to these strict decrees I'll write my name.

KING

How well your step back rescues you from shame. 120

BEROWNE *(reads)*

Article one: That no woman shall come within a mile of my

court. — Is this what it says?

LONGAVILLE

It was written four days ago.

BEROWNE

Let's see the penalty — *On pain of losing her cli* — . Who made
this up?   125

LONGAVILLE

That? O, that was I.

BEROWNE

Sweet lord, and why?

LONGAVILLE

To fright them all with that harsh penalty.

BEROWNE

A dangerous law against humanity.

Article two: If any man speaks to a woman within three years,   130
he shall endure such public shame as the rest of the court can
possibly propose.

This article, my king, you have to break,

For you yourself know that the French Princess

Comes with urgent business to speak with you —   135

A maid of grace and complete majesty —

About what's happening with Aquitaine

To her old, sick, and bedridden father:

Therefore this article will be made void,

Or the princess's purpose here is pointless.   140

KING

I forgot all about her. What should I do?

We must back up with this decree.

She must stay here: it's hospitality.

BEROWNE

Hospitality will make us all look dumb

Three thousand times within this three years' space;   145

For every man with his passions is born,

Not mastered by might, but by special grace.
If I break the oath, my word shall speak for me:
I lied "in the name of hospitality."
So on this document I sign my name,   150
And he that breaks these laws to any degree
Stands naked, an object of eternal shame.
This stands for you as it stands for me;
But believe, although I am so loath,
I'll be the last that will last keep his oath.   155

(Berowne signs)

What on earth shall we do to keep us tamed?

KING

Why this. Our court, you know, is patronized
By the renowned traveller of Spain,
A man with all the new world's present fashions,
That has a vault of phrases in his brain,   160
One whom the music of his own vain tongue
Raptures like some enchanting harmony,
An arrogant man, whose opinions
And thoughts concern no one but himself.
This child of fancy, Armado they call,   165
To entertain our scholars he'll "parlay"
With tales of knights whose enemies did fall
In tawny Spain, lost to the noble fray.
How you delight, good men, I know not, I,
But I protest his words fill me with glee,   170
And I will use him very mockingly.

BEROWNE

Armado is a most illustrious light,
A man of fire-new words, fashion's own knight.

LONGAVILLE

Costard, that clown! Ah! He shall be our sport,

7

So studying for three years will feel short.   175

Enter Dull the Constable, with a letter, and Costard

DULL

Which one of you is the king?

BEROWNE

This, fellow. What's wrong?

DULL

I'm his grace's parish officer. But I would see his own person
in flesh and blood.

BEROWNE

This is he.   180

DULL

Señor Arm … Arm … entreats you. There's trouble coming.
This letter will tell you more.

COSTARD

Sir, the letter is about me.

KING

A letter from the magnificent Armado.

BEROWNE

However low this is, I hope to God for high words.   185

LONGAVILLE

A high hope for a low heaven. Here we go!

BEROWNE

Are you ready to hear?

LONGAVILLE

To hear meekly, sir, and to laugh moderately, or neither.

BEROWNE

Well, I'm sure the style will give us cause for laughter.

COSTARD

The matter is the maid Jaquenetta. The manner of it is, I was 190
taken with the matter.

BEROWNE

In what manner?

COSTARD

Well. I was seen with her in the manor-house, sitting with
her upon the manor, and taken following her into the park.
Now, sir, for the manner: it is the manner of a man to speak   195
to a woman; for the matter: about some "matters."

BEROWNE

For the "following," sir?

COSTARD

As it shall follow!

KING

Let's hear this letter.

BEROWNE

As we would hear an oracle.   200

COSTARD

Some oracle!

KING *(reads)*

Great deputy, the heaven's second command, and sole dominator
of Navarre, my soul's earth's god and body's fostering patron —

COSTARD

Not a word of Costard yet.

KING

So it is —   205

COSTARD

If he says so … !

KING

Peace!

COSTARD

Be with me.

KING

No words!

9

COSTARD

Of other men's secrets. 210

KING

So it is, besieged with sable-coloured melancholy, I did com-
mend the black oppressing humour to the most wholesome
physic of thy health-giving air; and, as I am a gentleman, took
myself for a walk. The time, when? About the sixth hour, when
beasts most graze, birds best peck, and men sit down to that 215
nourishment which is called "supper." So much for the time
when. Now for the ground, which? Which, I mean, I walked
upon. It is called a "park". Then for the place, where? Where,
I mean, I did encounter that obscene and most preposterous
event that draweth from my snow-white pen the black-coloured 220
ink, which here thou viewest, beholdest, surveyest or seest. But
to the place, where? It standeth north-north-east and by east
from the west corner of thy curious-knotted garden. There did
I see that good for nothing bum, that bottomless pit of life —

COSTARD

Me? 225

KING

That unlettered small-knowing soul —

COSTARD

Me?

KING

That shallow wretch —

COSTARD

Not me.

KING

Which, as I remember, was Costard — 230

COSTARD

O, me!

KING

Companioned and consorted, contrary to thy established pro-
claimed mandate and celibate command, which with, O, with
— but I can barely speak what with —

COSTARD

With a maid.   235

KING

With a child of our grandmother Eve, a female, or, for thy more
sweet understanding, a woman. Him I, as my ever-esteemed
duty pricks me on, have sent to thee, to receive the need of pun-
ishment, by thy sweet grace's officer, Anthony Dull, a man of
good repute, carriage, bearing, and estimation.   240

DULL

Me. I am Anthony Dull.

KING

For Jaquenetta, so is the weaker vessel called which I appre-
hended with the aforesaid clown, I keep her as a vessel of the
law's fury, and shall, at the least of thy sweet notice, bring her
to trial. Thine in all compliments of devoted and heart-burning 245
heat of duty,

Don Adriano de Armado.

BEROWNE

That could have been better, but it was the best he could do.

KING

Yes, the best for the worst. But, sir, what do you say to this?

COSTARD

Sir, I confess the maid.   250

KING

Did you hear the proclamation?

COSTARD

I heard what it says, but I really don't understand it.

KING

It was proclaimed a year's imprisonment to be taken with a
maid.

COSTARD

I wasn't with a maid, sir: I was taken with a lady. 255

KING

Well, it was proclaimed lady.

COSTARD

This was no lady, neither, sir; she was a virgin.

KING

It is so varied too, for it was proclaimed virgin.

COSTARD

If it were, I deny her virginity: I was taken with a girl.

KING

This girl will not serve your turn, sir. 260

COSTARD

This girl will serve my turn, sir.

KING

Sir, I will pronounce your sentence: you shall fast a week with
bran and water.

COSTARD

I had rather pray a month with meat and porridge.

KING

And Don Armado shall be your keeper. 265

My Lord Berowne, see him delivered;

And go we, men, to put in practice that

Which you have all so strongly sworn.

Exit the King, Longaville, and Dumaine

BEROWNE

I swear to God and all the saints on earth

These oaths and laws will prove a waste of time. 270

Come along, sir.

COSTARD

I suffer for the truth, sir, for true it is, I was taken with Jaquenetta, and Jaquenetta is a true girl. There goes my luck, and till then, I sit with sorrow.

Exit all

ACT 1 ◆ SCENE 2

Enter Armado and Moth, his page

ARMADO

Boy, what sign is this when a man's spirit grows great with melancholy?

MOTH

A great sign, sir, that he will look sad.

ARMADO

Why, sadness is one and the same, dear child.

MOTH

No, no, O lord, sir, no. 5

ARMADO

How does one part sadness and melancholy, my tender juvenal?

MOTH

By working hard, my tough señor.

ARMADO

Why tough señor? Why tough señor?

MOTH

Why tender juvenal? Why tender juvenal?

ARMADO

I use it, tender juvenal, as a rightful *nombre* pertaining to 10 your youth, which they call tender.

MOTH

And I, tough señor, as a fitting title to your age, which we may name tough.

ARMADO

Pretty and able.

MOTH

What do you mean, sir? I pretty and my saying able, or I able,   15
and my saying pretty?

ARMADO

You pretty, because little.

MOTH

Little pretty, because little. Wherefore able?

ARMADO

And therefore able, because quick.

MOTH

Are you praising me, señor?   20

ARMADO

My praise is fitting.

MOTH

I will praise a fox with the same praise.

ARMADO

What, that a fox is ingenious?

MOTH

That a fox is quick.

ARMADO

I do say you are quick with your answers. It heats my blood.   25

MOTH

I am yours sir.

ARMADO

Then please do not cross me while at this academy.

MOTH *(aside)*

I love to cross him.

ARMADO

I have promised to study three years with the King.

MOTH

You may do it in an hour, sir. 30

ARMADO

Impossiblé.

MOTH

How much is two plus one?

ARMADO

I am bad at numbers. Save it for the barmaid.

MOTH

But you are a gentleman and a player, sir.

ARMADO

That I am. I am the example of a modern man. 35

MOTH

Then I am sure you know how much this amounts to.

ARMADO

It amounts to one more than two.

MOTH

Which the real people call "three."

ARMADO

True.

MOTH

So what's to study? You made it to three. And how easy it is 40
to put "years" to the word "three," and study three years in
two words.

ARMADO

Three. A most fine figure!

MOTH *(aside)*

To prove you're a zero.

ARMADO

Moth. I must confess: I am in love. And as it is wrong for a 45
soldier to love, so am I in love with the wrong woman. If I
could rip my heart out of my chest, I would take desire and

sell it to the highest bidder. I'm sighing — I feel pathetic!
Comfort me, boy. What great men have been in love?

MOTH

Hercules.   50

ARMADO

Hercules — too soft! Dear boy, name more. And, my sweet
child, let them be men of better honour and character.

MOTH

Samson. He was a man of good character, great character,
for he carried the town-gates on his back like a porter, and
he was in love.   55

ARMADO

O well-knit Samson, strong-jointed Samson! I am better with
the sword than you were at carrying gates. I am in love too.
Who was Samson's love, my dear Moth?

MOTH

A woman.

ARMADO

What kind of woman?   60

MOTH

All kinds of woman.

ARMADO

Tell me precisely of what temperament.

MOTH

Of the sea-water green, sir.

ARMADO

Is that the temperament of a lady?

MOTH

As I have read, sir, and the best of them too.   65

ARMADO

Green indeed is the colour of lovers. But to have a lover of
that colour, I think Samson had small reason for it. He surely

did love Delilah for her wit.

MOTH

It was so, sir, for she had a green wit.

ARMADO

My love is most impeccable white and red. 70

MOTH

Most peckable thought are masked under such colours.

ARMADO

What do you mean, define, well-educated infant.

MOTH

My father's wit and my mother's tongue assist me!

ARMADO

Spit it out, child!

MOTH

If she be made of white and red, 75

Her faults will ne'er be known,

For blushing cheeks by faults are bred,

And fears by pale white shown.

Then if she fear or be to blame,

By this you shall not know, 80

For still her cheeks possess the same

Which naturally she'll show.

A dangerous rhyme, señor, against the reason of white and red.

ARMADO

Is there not a ballad, boy, of the King and the Beggar?

MOTH

There was once a song like that before my time, but no one 85
knows it any more.

ARMADO

I will have the song rewritten, to prove that great men have
been in love before me. Moth, I do love that Jaquenetta, the
country girl that I accosted in the park with the rational boar

17

Costard. She deserves well. 90

MOTH *(aside)*

To be whipped? The whip would still be a better lover than he.

ARMADO

Sing. My spirit grows heavy in love.

I say sing!

MOTH

Wait till this company is passed.

Enter Costard, Dull, and Jaquenetta

DULL

Sir, the King's request is that you keep Costard safe; and you 95 must let him take no delight or solace, and he must fast three days a week. For this damsel, I must keep her at the park: she is sanctioned to serve the milkmaid. Farewell.

ARMADO *(aside)*

I feel my cheeks turning red. — Maid —

JAQUENETTA

Man. 100

ARMADO

I will see you at the lodge.

JAQUENETTA

That's close by.

ARMADO

I know exactly where it is.

JAQUENETTA

Oh, how wise you are!

ARMADO

I will tell you wonders. 105

JAQUENETTA

With that face?

ARMADO

I love you.

JAQUENETTA

So I heard you say.

ARMADO

And so farewell.

JAQUENETTA

Bye. 110

DULL

Come, Jaquenetta, away.

Exit Dull and Jaquenetta

ARMADO

Villain, you shall fast for your offences before you are set free.

COSTARD

Well, sir, I hope when I do it I shall do it on a full stomach.

ARMADO

You shall be heavily punished!

COSTARD

I am more bound to you than your fellows, for they are but 115
lightly rewarded.

ARMADO

Take away this villain. Lock him up.

MOTH

Come, you dirty bastard, away!

COSTARD

Let me not be pent up, sir, I will fast being loose.

MOTH

No, sir, you are fast and loose. You'll go to prison. 120

COSTARD

Well, if ever I do see the merry days of desolation that I have
seen, some shall see —

MOTH

What shall some see?

COSTARD

Nay, nothing, Moth, but what they look upon. It is wrong for
prisoners to be too silent in their words and therefore I will 125
say nothing. I thank God I have as little patience as another
man and therefore I can be quiet.

Exit Moth and Costard

ARMADO

I do affect the very ground, which is base, where her shoe,
which is baser, guided by her foot, which is basest, does
tread. I shall be forsworn, which is a great argument of false- 130
hood, if I love. And how can that be true love which is falsely
attempted? Love is a beast; Love is a devil. There is no evil
angel but Love. Yet Samson was so tempted, and he had an
excellent strength. Yet was Solomon so seduced, and he had
a very good wit. Cupid's arrow is too hard for Hercules's 135
club, and therefore too much odds for a Spaniard's rapier.
The first and second cause will not serve my turn. The thrust
he respects not; the swing he regards not. His disgrace is to
be called boy, but his glory is to subdue men. Adieu, valour;
rust, rapier; be still, drum, for your manager is in love. Yea, 140
he loveth. Assist me, some spontaneous god of rhyme, for I
am ready to turn sonneteer. Devise, wit; write, pen; for I am
for whole volumes in folio.

Exit

ACT 2 ◆ SCENE 1

Enter the Princess of France, with her ladies, Rosaline, Maria,
Katherine, and Lord Boyet, and another Lord

BOYET

Now, madam, summon up your dearest spirits.
Remember that the King, your father, sends
You. You, held precious in the world's esteem.
Remember to whom you're sent, and what's your plea:
To consult with the sole inheritor   5
Of all perfections that a man may owe:
Matchless Navarre. To claim no less prize
Than Aquitaine, a dowry for this queen.
Hold to your abundance of all grace
As Nature was in making graces dear   10
When she did starve the general world outside
And prodigally gave all grace to you.

PRINCESS

Good Lord, Boyet, my beauty, though but plain,
Needs not the painted flourish of your praise.
Beauty is bought by judgement of the eye,   15
Not uttered by base sale of merchant tongues.
I am less proud to hear you tell my worth
Than you are proud in being counted wise
In spending your wit in the praise of mine.
But now to task the tasker. Good Boyet,   20
You are not ignorant to the gossip here
That this "matchless" Navarre has made a vow,
Till painful study shall outwear three years,
No woman may approach his silent court.

Therefore, to us it seems a needful course, 25
Before we enter his "forbidden" gates,
To know his pleasure; and in that behalf,
Sure of your worthiness, we single you
As our best-moving, fair good messenger.
Tell him the daughter, the Princess of France, 30
On serious business craving quick dispatch,
Demands a personal conference with his grace.
Go, signify that much, while we attend,
Like humble-beautied suitors, his high will.

BOYET

Proud of employment, willingly I go. 35

PRINCESS

All pride is willing pride, and yours is so.

Exit Boyet

Who are these disciples, my loving maids,
That are vow-fellows with this virtuous King?

A LORD

Longaville is one.

PRINCESS

Know you the man? 40

MARIA

I met him, madam. At a marriage feast
In Normandy, I saw this Longaville.
A man of virtuous heart, he is esteemed,
Well fitted in arts, glorious in arms.
Everything he touches turns to gold. 45
The only soil of his fair virtue's shine —
If virtue's shine will stain with any soil —
Is a sharp wit matched with too blunt a will.
His wit has power to cut, while his will wills
None will be spared that come within his power. 50

22

PRINCESS

 Some merry mocking lord, it seems: is it so?

MARIA

 They say so most that most his humours know.

PRINCESS

 Such short-lived wits do wither as they grow.

 Tell me the rest.

KATHERINE

 The young Dumaine, a well-accomplished youth,   55

 All who love virtue love his virtuous heart;

 He is the strongest of all three, but knows the least

 For he has skill to make a cruel shape kind,

 And shape to win grace, even if he had no wit.

 I saw him at the Duke Alençon's once;   60

 And much too little of that good I saw.

 There is more to his great worthiness.

ROSALINE

 Another of these students at that time

 Was there with him, if I have heard a truth.

 Berowne they call him, but a merrier man,   65

 Just within the limit of being uncouth,

 I never spent an hour's talk with him.

 For every object that one eye catches

 The other turns to a mirth-moving joke.

 His eyes create occasion for his wit,   70

 While his fair tongue, conceit's interpreter,

 Delivers in such quick and gracious words

 That older ears are repulsed by his tales

 And younger hearings are quite ravished:

 So smart and eloquent is his discourse.   75

PRINCESS

 God bless these ladies! Are they all in love,

That every one her own has embellished
With such bedecking ornaments of praise?

MARIA

Here comes Boyet.

Enter Boyet

PRINCESS

Now, what good news, my lord?   80

BOYET

The King had notice of your fair approach,
And he and his fellow-scholars in oath
Were all addressed to meet you, gentle lady,
Before I came. Indeed, this much I have learned:
He rather means to keep you in the field,   85
Like one that comes here to besiege his court,
Than seek a relaxation from his oath,
To let you enter his unpeopled house.

Enter King Ferdinand, Berowne,
Longaville, and Dumaine

Here comes the King.

KING

Fair Princess, welcome to the court of Navarre.   90

PRINCESS

"Fair" I give you back again, and "welcome" I have not yet.
The roof of this court is too high to be yours, and welcome to
the wide fields too cheap to be mine.

KING

You are welcome here, madam, to my court.

PRINCESS

I will be welcomed then. Now take me there.   95

KING

Hear me, dear lady: I have sworn an oath.

24

PRINCESS

Our Lady help this man! He'll break his oath.

KING

Not for the world, fair madam, by my will.

PRINCESS

Why, will shall break it; will, and nothing else.

KING

Your ladyship is ignorant —   100

PRINCESS

O my lord let your ignorance be wise,

For now his knowledge must prove ignorance.

I hear your grace has sworn out housekeeping.

It's deadly sin to keep that oath, my lord,

And sin to break it.   105

But pardon me, I am too sudden bold;

To teach a King does not here suit a Queen.

Please read this purpose of my arrival

And suddenly resolve me in my quest.

She gives the King a paper

KING

Madam, I will, if suddenly I may.   110

PRINCESS

You would prefer that soon I went away,

For you'll prove perjured if you make me stay.

The King reads

BEROWNE *(to Rosaline)*

Did I not dance beneath your stockings once?

· ROSALINE

Did you not dance beneath my stockings once?

BEROWNE

Indeed I did.   115

25

ROSALINE

How needless was it then

To ask the question!

BEROWNE

You must not be so quick.

ROSALINE

You bore me with your questions.

BEROWNE

Your tongue's too hot, it speeds too fast, you must. 120

ROSALINE

Not till it leave the rider in the dust.

BEROWNE

When did we play?

ROSALINE

What a foolish thought.

BEROWNE

Those are the stockings that I bought!

ROSALINE

Watch your tongue, you thoughtless beast. 125

BEROWNE

I'll tame mine at the very least.

ROSALINE

Goodbye, I'm done.

BEROWNE

Not before I'm gone.

He leaves her

KING

Madam, your father in this letter claims

That he repaid my hundred thousand crowns, 130

Which is only one half of the entire sum

Loaned by my father to fund your father's war.

To say that we have ever received that sum

From France is not all true — and still you owe
A hundred thousand more! Until he pays,   135
His crownless Aquitaine belongs to me,
Although he knows it's not worth half the sum.
If your frail father would simply pay half,
The debt which still remains unsatisfied,
We will give up our right in Aquitaine   140
And hold fair friendship with his majesty.
My grace in this event has been ignored:
For here he does outrageously demand
A hundred thousand crowns, and offers not
To pay me my one hundred thousand more,   145
So he can have his Aquitaine returned.
In short, we truly would much rather have
The money that my royal father lent,
Than worthless Aquitaine, that crippled land.
Dear princess, were not his requests so far   150
From human reason, your fair self might dull
Sharp Reason's blade that lies within my breast
And lead you back to France well satisfied.

PRINCESS

You do the King my father too much wrong
And wrong the reputation of your name,   155
In so refusing to confess receipt
Of that which has so faithfully been paid.

KING

I do protest I never heard of it.
And, if you prove it, I'll repay it back
Or renounce Aquitaine.   160

PRINCESS

We accept your word.
Boyet, where is the evidence

27

For such a sum from special officers
Of Charles, his father?

KING

Satisfy me so.   165

BOYET

So please your grace, the packet is not come
Where that and other specialties are bound.
Tomorrow you shall have a sight of them.

KING

It shall suffice me; at which juncture I
Will yield unto all liberal reasons.   170
Meanwhile, receive this welcome at my hand
As honour, without breach of oath, may here
Uphold your own majesty in my house.
You may not come, fair Princess, within my gates,
But in this field you shall be so received   175
As you shall deem yourself lodged in my heart,
Though so denied fair harbour in my house.
Your own good thoughts excuse me, and farewell.
Tomorrow we shall visit you again.

PRINCESS

Sweet health and fair desires go with your grace.   180

KING

Your own wish wish I you in every place.

Exit the King, Longaville, and Dumaine

BEROWNE

Lady, I will confide you to my own heart.

ROSALINE

Pray you, send my regards; I would be glad to see it.

BEROWNE

I would you heard it moan.

ROSALINE

Is the fool sick? 185

BEROWNE

Sick at the heart.

ROSALINE

Of course, let it bleed.

BEROWNE

Would that do it good?

ROSALINE

My physic says ay.

BEROWNE

Will you prick it with your eye? 190

ROSALINE

No sir, with my knife.

BEROWNE

Now God save your life.

ROSALINE

And yours from long living.

BEROWNE

I can't take what you're giving.

Exit

Enter Dumaine

DUMAINE

Sir, I pray you a word. What lady is that same? 195

BOYET

The heir of Alençon, Katherine's her name.

DUMAINE

A handsome lady. Monsieur, farewell.

Exit

Enter Longaville

LONGAVILLE

You, a word. Who is she in the white?

BOYET

A woman sometimes, if you saw her in the light.

LONGAVILLE

I desire her name. 200

BOYET

She has but one for herself; to desire that were a shame.

LONGAVILLE

Whose daughter is she?

BOYET

Her mother's, I have heard.

LONGAVILLE

O God, sir, use your words!

BOYET

Good sir, be not offended. 205

She is an heir of Falconbridge.

LONGAVILLE

Hmm, my anger has ended.

She is a most sweet lady.

BOYET

Not unlike, sir, that may be.

Exit Longaville

Enter Berowne

BEROWNE

What's her name in the cap? 210

BOYET

Rosaline, perhaps.

BEROWNE

Is she wedded or no?

BOYET

To her will sir, or so.

BEROWNE

You are welcome, sir. Adieu.

BOYET

Farewell to me, sir, and welcome to you.   215

Exit Berowne

MARIA

That last is Berowne, the lovely lowbrow'd lord.

Not a word with him except a jest.

BOYET

And every jest a word.

PRINCESS

It was well done of you to take him at his word.

BOYET

I was as willing to sail off as he was to board.   220

MARIA

You are a departing ship, man!

BOYET

And wherefore not "ships"?

No ship, sweet lamb, unless we feed on your lips.

MARIA

You lamb, and I pasture. Shall that finish the jest?

BOYET

So you grant pasture for me.   225

He tries to kiss her

MARIA

Not so, gentle beast.

My lips are no common, though several they be.

BOYET

Belonging to whom?

MARIA

To my fortunes and me.

PRINCESS

Your wits will be chattering; but, gentles, agree.   230

This civil war of wits were much better used

31

On the King and his bookmen, for here it's abused.

BOYET

If my observation, which very rarely lies

I see the truth of his heart shining through his eyes,

Don't deceive me, the King has an infection.   235

PRINCESS

With what?

BOYET

With that which we lovers entitle "affection."

PRINCESS

Your reasoning?

BOYET

Well, all his behaviours they did conspire

To the court of his eye, poking through with desire.   240

His heart, like a ruby with your print impressed,

Proud with his form, in his eye pride expressed.

His tongue, all impatient to speak and not see,

Did stumble with haste in his eyesight to be.

All senses to that sense did find their way there,   245

To feel only looking on fairest of fair.

I thought all his senses were locked in his eye,

As jewels in crystal for some prince to buy;

But working as hard as he can on his oath

His eyes saw his eye and fell victim to "growth."   250

His face's own margin did quote such amazes

That all eyes saw his eyes enchanted with gazes.

He'll give you Aquitaine, and all that is his,

If you give him for our sake but one loving kiss.

PRINCESS

Come to our pavilion. Boyet is quite mad.   255

BOYET

But to speak that in words which had made his heart glad.

I only have made a mouth of his eye

By adding a tongue which I know will not lie.

MARIA

You are an old love-monger, and speak skillfully.

KATHERINE

He is Cupid's grandfather, and learns news of him. 260

ROSALINE

Then was Venus like her mother, for her father is just grim.

BOYET

Do you hear, my mad wenches?

MARIA

No.

BOYET

What then, do you see?

KATHERINE

Yes, our way to be gone. 265

BOYET

You are too harsh for me.

Exit all

ACT 3 ◆ SCENE 1

Enter Armado and Moth

ARMADO

Sing me a song, Moth, my ears lust for some music.

MOTH

Sings "When Colinet ..."

ARMADO

Sweet air! Go, tenderness of years, take this key, and release
Costard, that dunce. Bring him here at a gallop's pace! For he
is to dispatch a letter to my love.

MOTH

Señor, will you win your love with your French tongue?   5

ARMADO

What do you mean? Tonguing in French?

MOTH

No, my complete master; but to jig off a tune at the tongue's
end, tippy-toe to it with your feet, humour it with closing
your eyelids, sigh a high note and sing a low note, sometimes
through the throat as if you swallowed love with singing love,   10
with your hat tilted down over the top of your eyes, with your
arms crossed on your thin-belly vest like a penguin with a
stick, or your hands in your pocket like a man in an old
painting rocking back and forth; and keep not too long in
one tune, but a snip and away. These are suggestions, these   15
are ideas, these will bewitch nice maids; and make legends of
men that most behave like this.

ARMADO

How have you gathered this experience?

MOTH

By observation.

ARMADO

Bring Costard here. He must carry me a letter.   20

The way is short. Away!

MOTH

As swift as lead, sir.

ARMADO

"Swift as lead." Your meaning seems null.

Is lead not a heavy metal, slow and dull?

MOTH

Non, honest señor; or rather, señor, no.   25

ARMADO

I say lead is slow.

MOTH

You are too swift, sir, to say so.

Is that lead slow which is fired from a gun?

ARMADO

I shoot you at Costard, go!

MOTH

Shoot then, and I flee.   30

Exit

ARMADO

A most sharp youth, articulate and free of grace!

By your favour, sweet heavens, I must sigh in your face.

Chivalric courage, melancholy has taken your place.

My herald is returned.

Enter Moth and Costard

MOTH

A wonder, master! Here's a costard with a broken shin.   35

ARMADO

Some enigma, some riddle. Come, explain — begin.

COSTARD

No eggs, no riddle, no ending, no salve in your letter, sir! O, sir, wolfsbane, a plain wolfsbane! No ending, no ending, no salve, sir, but wolfsbane!

ARMADO

By virtue, you enforce laughter; your silly thought, my spleen; 40 the heaving of my lungs provokes me to ridiculous smiling. O, pardon me, my stars! Slippery Costard, I will emancipate you

COSTARD

O, marry me to one with French eyes! I smell some ending, some goose in this. 45

ARMADO

By my sweet soul, I mean setting you at liberty, enfreedoming your person. You were immured, restrained, captivated, bound.

COSTARD

True, true, and now will you be my liberator, and let me loose.

ARMADO

I give you your liberty, set you from penance, and in lieu 50 thereof impose on you nothing but this: *(Armado gives Costard a letter)* bear this letter to the country maid Jaquenetta. There is remuneration *(he gives Costard a coin)*, for the best prize of my honour is to reward my dependents. Moth, follow.

Exit

MOTH

Like the sequel, I. Signior Costard, adieu. 55

Exit

COSTARD

My sweet ounce of man's flesh, my rare juvenal! Now will I look to his remuneration. "Remuneration!" O, that's the Latin word for three farthings. Three farthings — remuner-

ation. "What's the price of this trifle?" "One penny." "No, I'll
give you a remuneration." Why, it carries it. "Remuneration!" 60
Why, it is a fairer name than French crown. I will never buy
and sell without using this word.

Enter Berowne

BEROWNE

My good man Costard, exceedingly well met.

COSTARD

Pray you, sir, how much carnation ribbon may a man buy for
a remuneration? 65

BEROWNE

What is a "remuneration"?

COSTARD

Well, sir, three farthings.

BEROWNE

Why then, three-farthings-worth of silk.

COSTARD

I thank your worship. Goodbye.

BEROWNE

Stay, clown. I must employ you. 70

Do one thing for me that I shall entreat.

And you will win my favour, good my friend.

COSTARD

When would you have it done, sir?

BEROWNE

This afternoon.

COSTARD

Well, I will do it, sir. Farewell. 75

BEROWNE

You don't know what it is.

COSTARD

I shall know, sir, when I have done it.

BEROWNE

Why, dummy, you must know first.

COSTARD

I will come to your worship tomorrow morning.

BEROWNE

It must be done this afternoon. 80

Wait, clown, it is but this:

The Princess comes to hunt here in the park,

And in her train there is a gentle lady;

When tongues speak sweetly, then they name her name,

And Rosaline they call her. Ask for her 85

And put in her fair hand

This sealed-up counsel.

(Berowne gives Costard a letter)

Here's your payment: go.

(he gives Costard money)

COSTARD

Payment, O sweet payment! Better than remuneration,
eleven and twelve farthings better. Most sweet payment! I 90
will do it, sir, in print. Payment! Remuneration!

Exit

BEROWNE

Dear God, I'm in love! I, that have whipped love out of men,

I, a very warden to a lover's sigh,

I, a critic, nay, I, a night-watch constable,

I, a domineering pedant over that boy, 95

Than whom no mortal is more arrogant!

That masked, whining, blinded, wayward boy,

That Senior Junior, giant dwarf, Dan Cupid,

Ruler of love-rhymes, lord of folded arms,

The anointed emperor of sighs and moans, 100

King of all loiterers and malcontents,

The prince of stockings, king of codpieces,
Sole imperator and great general
Of trotting whoremongers — O my little heart! —
And I to be a corporal of his field   105
And wave his flag like an old ringmaster!
What? I love, I sue, I seek a wife?
This woman that is like a wily fox,
Needs grooming, taming, ever out of line
And never going aright, being a beast,   110
Wanting eyes on her hoping she'll do right!
No, to be perjured, which is worst of all;
And among three to love the worst of all;
A wilful wanton with a velvet brow,
With two bright jewels stuck in her face for eyes;   115
Yes, and by heaven, one that will do the deed
Though Boyet is her guard with a hundred eyes.
And I to sigh for her, to watch for her,
To pray for her! Damnit, it is a plague
That Cupid will impose for my neglect   120
Of his almighty dreadful little might.
Well, I will love, write, sigh, pray, sue, and groan.
Some men can't love a lady, but I'm Berowne.

Exit

ACT 4 ◆ SCENE 1

Enter the Princess, a Forester, Rosaline, Maria,
Katherine, and Boyet

PRINCESS

Was that the king that drove his horse so hard

Against the steep uprising of the hill?

BOYET

I don't know, but I don't think it was him.

PRINCESS

Whoever he was, he showed ambitious mind.

Well, lords, today we shall be well dismissed;　　　　　5

On Saturday we will return to France.

Then, forester, my friend, where is the bush

That we must stand and slay the wild deer in?

FORESTER

Near here, upon the edge of that grove,

Stand here so you may make the fairest shoot.　　　　　10

PRINCESS

I thank my beauty, I am fair that shoot,

And thereupon you call me "the fairest shoot."

FORESTER

Pardon me, madam, for I did not mean so.

PRINCESS

What, what? First praise me, and again say no?

O, short-lived pride! Not fair? You should go!　　　　　15

FORESTER

Yes, madam, fair.

PRINCESS

No, don't applaud me now.

41

Where fair is not, praise cannot mend the brow.
Here, my good man, take this for telling true:
(she gives the Forester money)
Fair payment for foul words is more than due.   20
FORESTER
Nothing but fair is that which you inherit.

Exit

PRINCESS
See, see, my beauty will be saved by merit!
O blasphemy in words, unfit for days!
A giving hand, though foul, shall have fair praise.
But come, the bow. Now mercy goes to kill,   25
And shooting well is then accounted ill.
Thus will I save my credit in the shoot:
Not wounding, 'pity would not let me do't';
If wounding, then it was to show my skill,
That more for praise than purpose meant to kill.   30
And out of question so it is sometimes,
Glory grows guilty of detested crimes,
When for fame's sake, for praise, that outward part,
We bend to that the working of the heart;
As I for praise alone now seek to spill   35
The poor deer's blood, that my heart means no ill.
BOYET
Do not cursed wives hold that authority
Only for praise' sake, when they strive to be
Lords over their lords?
PRINCESS
Only for praise, and praise we may afford   40
To any lady that subdues a lord.

Enter Costard with a letter

BOYET

Here comes the king of the common folk.

COSTARD

God bless you all! I ask who is the head lady?

PRINCESS

You will know her, fellow, by the rest that have no heads.

COSTARD

Which is the greatest lady, the highest?   45

PRINCESS

The thickest and the tallest.

COSTARD

The thickest and the tallest. It is so, truth is truth.

If your waist, mistress, were as slender as my wit,

One of these maids' girdles for your waist should be fit.

Are not you the chief woman? You are the thickest here.   50

PRINCESS

What's your will, sir? What's your will?

COSTARD

I have a letter from Monsieur Berowne to one Lady Rosaline.

PRINCESS

Ooh, your letter, your letter! He's a good friend of mine.

(she takes the letter)

Stand aside, good messenger. Boyet, you can open:

Break up this seal.   55

BOYET

I am bound to serve.

(Boyet examines the letter)

This letter is mistook: it is not for anyone here.

It is written for Jaquenetta.

PRINCESS

We will read it, go on.

Break the neck of the wax, and everyone give ear.   60

BOYET *(reads)*

> By heaven, that thou art fair is most infallible; true that thou
> art beauteous; truth itself that thou art lovely. More fairer than
> fair, beautiful than beauteous, truer than truth itself, have
> commiseration on thy heroical service. The magnanimous and
> most illustrate King David set eye upon the pernicious and   65
> undoubted beggar Bathsheba, and he it was that might rightly
> say, Veni, vidi, vici, which to anatomize in the vulgar, — O
> base and obscure vulgar! — that is, he came, see, and over-
> came. He came, one; see, two; overcame, three. Who came? The
> King. Why did he come? To see. Why did he see? To overcome.   70
> To whom came he? To the beggar. What saw he? The beggar.
> Who overcame he? The beggar. The conclusion is victory. On
> whose side? The King's. The captive is enriched. On whose side?
> The beggar's. The denouement is a wedding. On whose side?
> The King's? No, on both in one, or one in both. I am the King,   75
> for so stands the comparison, thou the beggar, for so witnesseth
> thy lowliness. Shall I command thy love? I may. Shall I enforce
> thy love? I could. Shall I entreat thy love? I will. What shalt
> thou exchange for rags? Robes. For tittles? Titles. For thyself?
> Me. Thus expecting thy reply, I profane my lips on thy foot, my   80
> eyes on thy picture, and my heart on thy every part.
> Thine in the dearest design of industry,
> Don Adriano de Armado.
> Thus dost thou hear the Nemean lion roar
> 'Gainst thee, thou lamb, that standest as his prey.   85
> Submissive fall his princely feet before,
> And he from hunting will incline to play.
> But if thou fight, poor soul, what art thou then?
> Food for his rage, a feasting for his den.

PRINCESS

What peacock is he that inked this letter?   90

What vain? What rascal? Did you ever hear better?

BOYET

I am much deceived but I remember the style.

PRINCESS

Else your memory is bad, we haven't heard it for a while.

BOYET

This Armado is a Spaniard that keeps here in court,

A madman, a deluded one, and one that makes sport   95

To the Prince and his book-mates.

PRINCESS

You, Costard, a word.

Who gave you this letter?

COSTARD

I told you: my lord.

PRINCESS

Who was this intended for?   100

COSTARD

From my lord to my lady.

PRINCESS

From which lord to which lady?

COSTARD

From my lord Berowne, a good master of mine,

To a lady of France that he called Rosaline.

PRINCESS

You have mistaken his letter. Come, lords, away.   105

(to Rosaline)

Here, sweet, put up this: it'll be yours another day.

> *Exit all but Boyet, Rosaline, Maria, and Costard*

BOYET

Who is the shooter? Who is the shooter?

ROSALINE

Shall I teach you to know?

BOYET

You, my continent of beauty.

ROSALINE

Why, she that bears the bow.   110

Finely put off!

BOYET

My lady goes to kill deer, but if you marry,

Hang me by the neck, if deer that year miscarry.

Finely put on!

ROSALINE

Well, then, I am the shooter.   115

BOYET

And who is your shot?

ROSALINE

If we choose by the combs, yourself come not near.

Finely put on indeed!

MARIA

You still wrangle with her, Boyet, and she strikes at the brow.

BOYET

But she herself is hit lower. Have I hit her now?   120

ROSALINE

Must I jest with you in sayings as old as Charlemagne, that

men like you might hit it?

BOYET

So I may answer thee with one as old as Guinevere, such that

a woman can hit it.

ROSALINE

You cannot hit it, hit it, hit it,   125

You cannot hit it, my good man.

BOYET

If I cannot, cannot, cannot,

If I cannot, another can.

46

Exit Rosaline

COSTARD

How great was that! How both did fit it!

MARIA

A mark incredibly well shot, for they both did hit it.   130

BOYET

A mark! Hey, look at that mark! A mark, says my lady.

Let the mark have a buck in't, to aim at, if it may be.

MARIA

Wide of the bow hand! Indeed your hand is dark.

COSTARD

Indeed, he must shoot nearer, or he'll never hit the mark.

BOYET

If my hand be out, then surely your hand is in.   135

COSTARD

Then will she get the best shot by hitting the pin.

MARIA

Come, come, you talk greasily, your lips grow foul.

COSTARD

She's too hard for you at bucks, sir. Challenge her to bowl.

BOYET

I fear too much rubbing. Good night, my good owl.

Exit Boyet and Maria

COSTARD

By my soul, a fool, a most simple clown!   140

Lord, Lord, how the ladies and I have put him down!

Oh my gosh, how funny, my excellent wit,

When it comes so smoothly off, so obscenely, as it were, so fit.

Armado on the other hand — Ugh, a most girlish man!

To see him walk before a lady and to bear her fan!   145

To see him kiss his hand, and how most sweetly he will swear!

And his page beside him, that handful of wit!

47

By heaven, he is most pathetical twit!

(shout within)

Coming, coming!

Exit

ACT 4 ♦ SCENE 2

Enter Dull, Holofernes the Pedant, and Nathaniel the Curate

NATHANIEL

Very refined sport, truly, and done in the spirit of good conscience.

HOLOFERNES

The deer was, as you know, dripping in blood, ripe as the pomegranate, who now hangs like a jewel in the ear of the sky, the heaven, the firmament and soon falls like a crab on 5 the face of the soil, the land, the earth.

NATHANIEL

Truly, Master Holofernes, the epithets are sweetly varied, like a scholar at the least: but, sir, I assure ye it was a buck in its prime.

HOLOFERNES

Sir Nathaniel, I don't believe that. 10

DULL

It not a "limp old rooster," it was a young buck.

HOLOFERNES

Most barbarous intimation! Yet a kind of insinuation, as it were, by way of explanation, as it were, replication, or rather to show, as it were, his inclination, after his undressed, unpolished, uneducated, unpruned, untrained, or rather 15 unlettered, or ratherest unconfirmed fashion, to insert again my disbelief for a buck.

Enter Jaquenetta with a letter and Costard

48

JAQUENETTA

God give you good morrow, Master Person.

NATHANIEL

Master Person, you mean pierce-one? And if one should be
pierced, which is the one?   20

COSTARD

Yes, Master Schoolmaster, he that is most like a hogshead.

HOLOFERNES

"Of piercing a hogshead"? A good flash of wit for a turf of
earth, fire enough for a cold flint, pearl enough for a swine:
it is pretty, it is well.

JAQUENETTA

Good Master Parson, be so good as read me this letter. It was   25
given to me by Costard and sent me from Don Armado. I
can't read it.

HOLOFERNES

Under pardon, sir, what are the contents? Or rather as Horace
says in his — what, my soul, verses?

NATHANIEL

Yes, sir, and very learned.   30

HOLOFERNES

Let me hear a staff, a stanza, a verse. Read, master.

NATHANIEL *(reads)*

If love make me forsworn, how shall I swear to love?
Ah, never faith could hold, if not to beauty vowed.
Though to myself forsworn, to you I'll faithful prove.
Those thoughts to me were oaks, to you like willows bowed.   35
These studies I will leave, and makes my book your eyes,
Where all those pleasures live, that art would comprehend.
If knowledge be the mark, to know you shall suffice:
Well learned is that tongue, that well can you commend,
All ignorant that soul, that sees you without wonder;   40

49

Which is to me some praise, that I your parts admire.
Your eye Jove's lightning bears, your voice his dreadful thunder,
Which, not to anger bent, is music and sweet fire.
Celestial as you are, O, pardon love this wrong,
That sings heaven's praise, with such an earthly tongue. 45

HOLOFERNES

You find not the apostrophe and so miss the accent. Let me supervise the canzonet. *(he takes the letter)* Here is only meter ratified, but for the elegancy, facility, and golden cadence of poesy, it is wanting. Ovidius Naso was the man; and why indeed "Naso," but for smelling out the odoriferous flowers 50 of fancy, the witty speeches of invention? To imitate is nothing. So does the hound his master, the ape his keeper, the tired horse his rider. But, damsella virgin, was this directed to you?

JAQUENETTA

Yes, sir, from one Monsieur Berowne, one of the strange 55 queen's lords.

HOLOFERNES

I will overglance the superscript: *To the fairest hand of the most beauteous Lady Rosaline.* I will look again on the intellect of the letter, for the nomination of the party writing to the person written unto: *Your Ladyship's in all desired employment,* 60 *Berowne.* Sir Nathaniel, this Berowne is one of the students of the King, and here he has framed a letter to a follower of the stranger queen's, which accidentally, or by the way of progression, has got lost. Trip and go, my sweet, deliver this paper into the royal hand of the King, it may concern much. 65 Stay not for compliment: I forgive your duty, adieu.

JAQUENETTA

Good Costard, go with me. Sir, God save your life.

COSTARD

I'm with you, my girl.

Exit Costard and Jaquenetta

NATHANIEL

Sir, you have done this in the fear of God, very religiously; and as a certain father says —   70

HOLOFERNES

Sir, tell me not of the father, I do fear a trunkful of wit. But to return to the verses: did they please you, Sir Nathaniel?

NATHANIEL

Marvellous penmanship.

HOLOFERNES

I do dine today at the father's of a certain pupil of mine, where if, before the meal, it shall please you to gratify the table with   75 a grace, I will, on my privilege I have with the parents of the foresaid child or pupil, undertake your welcome; where I will prove those verses to be very unlearned, neither savouring of poetry, wit, nor invention. I seek your society.

NATHANIEL

And thank you too, for society, says the text, is the happiness   80 of life.

HOLOFERNES

And certainly, the text most infallibly concludes it. *(to Dull)* Sir, I do invite you too: you shall not say no to me. Few words. Away, the gentlefolk are at their game, and we will to our recreation.   85

Exit all

ACT 4 ◆ SCENE 3

Enter Berowne with a paper in his hand, alone

BEROWNE

The King, is hunting deer; while I am killing myself. They

have pitched a toil; and I toiling in a pitch, pitch that defiles.
Defile, a foul word. Ugh, stop it with this sorrow, Berowne!
Sorrow is what the fool says, and thus I, being in sorrow, am
the fool. Well proved, wit! By the Lord, this love of mine is as 5
mad as a fox. It kills sheep, it kills me — I a sheep. Well, there
goes my wit again! I will not love; if I do, hang me! In faith, I
will not. O, but her eye! By this light, but for her eye, I would
not love her — yes, for her two eyes. Well, I do nothing in the
world but lie, and lie in my throat. By heaven, I do love, and 10
it has taught me to rhyme, and to be melancholy. And here
is part of my rhyme, and here my melancholy. Well, she has
one of my sonnets already. The fool bore it, the clown sent it,
and the lady has it. Sweet clown, sweeter fool, sweetest lady!
By the world, I would not care if the other three were in these 15
woods … watching. Here comes one, with a paper. God give
him grace to groan!

He stands aside

Enter the King with a paper

KING

Good grief!

BEROWNE

HA! by heaven the king's been shot! Proceed, sweet Cupid,
you've stuck him with your golden arrow under his left 20
breast. Now, I wait to hear him spill his secrets!

KING *(reads)*

So sweet a kiss the golden sun gives note
To those fresh morning drops upon the rose,
As your eye-beams when their fresh rays have smote
The night of dew that on my cheeks down flows. 25
Nor shines the silver moon one half so bright
Through the transparent bosom of the deep
As does your face, through tears of mine, give light.

Your face shines in every tear that I weep,
Each drop but as a carriage holding thee: 30
So must you rejoice in my awful woe,
And behold the tears that swell in me,
Your glory through my grief will show.
If you keep your love to yourself: then keep
My tears in glasses, and make me weep.   35
O Queen of queens, how far dost thou excel,
No thought can think, nor tongue of mortal tell.
How shall she know my griefs? I'll drop this paper.
Sweet page confess my folly. Who comes here?

The King steps aside

Enter Longaville with a paper

What, Longaville, and reading? Listen, ear!   40

BEROWNE

Now, in your likeness, one more fool appear!

LONGAVILLE

Why me? I am forsworn!

BEROWNE

Why, he comes in like a liar, wearing papers.

KING

In love, I hope. Sweet fellowship in shame!

BEROWNE

One drunkard loves another of the name.   45

LONGAVILLE

Am I the first to break my holy oath?

BEROWNE

I could put him out of his misery.
He is the third, the poor three-cornered cap of shame,
The shape of Love's gallows, that hang up simplicity.

LONGAVILLE

I fear these stubborn lines lack power to move.   50

O sweet Maria, empress of my love,
These numbers will I tear and write in prose.

BEROWNE

O, rhymes are poking through this fellow's hose:
Disfigure not his parts!

LONGAVILLE

This same shall go. 55

(he reads the sonnet)

Did not the heavenly rhetoric of your eye,
Against whom the world can't hold argument,
Persuade my heart to this false filthy lie?
Broken vows for you deserve not punishment.
A woman I swore off, but I will prove, 60
You being a goddess, I forswore not thee.
My vow was earthly, yours a heavenly love;
Your grace being gained, cures all disgrace in me.
Vows are but breath, and breath a vapour is:
Then you, fair sun, which on my earth does shine, 65
Dissolve this vapour-vow; in you it is.
If broken then, it is no fault of mine:
If broke by me, what fool is not so wise
To lose an oath to win a paradise?

BEROWNE

This is the lover's strain, which makes flesh a deity, 70
A strumpet queen to reign. Pure, pure idolatry.
God amend us, God amend! We are much out of the way.

Enter Dumaine with a paper

LONGAVILLE

By whom shall I send this? Company? Stay.

Longaville stands aside

BEROWNE

All hid, all hid, an old infant play.

Like a demi-god here sit I in the sky,   75
And wretched fools' secrets heedfully I eye.
More lies to find. O heavens, I have my wish!
Dumaine transformed! Four woodpeckers in a dish!

DUMAINE

O most divine Kate!

BEROWNE

O most noble idiot!   80

DUMAINE

By heaven, the wonder of a mortal eye!

BEROWNE

By earth, she's not, she's basic: there you lie.

DUMAINE

Her amber hairs for foul has amber quoted.

BEROWNE

An amber-coloured raven was well noted.

DUMAINE

As upright as the cedar.   85

BEROWNE

Stoop, I say.
Her shoulder is with child.

DUMAINE

As fair as day.

BEROWNE

Yes, as some days, but then no sun must shine.

DUMAINE

O that I had my wish!   90

LONGAVILLE

And I had mine!

KING

And I mine too, good Lord!

BEROWNE

Amen, so I had mine! Is not that a good word?

DUMAINE

I would forget her, but a fever she

Reigns in my blood and will remembered be. 95

BEROWNE

A fever in his blood? Why then incision

Would let her out in saucers. Sweet resolution!

DUMAINE

Once more I'll read the ode that I have penned.

BEROWNE

Once more I'll mark how love can wit attend.

DUMAINE *(Dumaine reads his sonnet)*

On a day — alack the day! — 100
Love, whose month is ever May,
Spied a blossom passing fair
Playing in the wanton air.
Through the velvet leaves the wind,
All unseen, can passage find; 105
That the lover, sick to death,
Wish himself the heaven's breath.
"Air," says he, "your cheeks may blow,
Air, would I might triumph so!
But, alack, my hand is sworn 110
Never to pluck you from your thorn.
Vow, alack, for youth unmeet,
Youth so right to pluck a sweet.
Do not call it sin in me,
That I am forsworn for thee; 115
Thou for whom Jove would swear
Juno but an Ethiop were,
And deny himself for Jove,

Turning mortal for thy love."
This will I send, and something else more plain,   120
That shall express my true love's fasting pain.
O, would the king, Berowne, and Longaville
Were lovers too! Ill, to example ill,
Would from my forehead wipe a lying note,
For none offend where all alike do dote.   125

LONGAVILLE *(comes forward)*

Dumaine, your love is far from charity,
That in love's grief desires society.
You may look pale, but I should blush, I know,
To be overheard and taken napping so.

KING *(comes forward)*

Come, sir, you blush. As his your case is such,   130
You chide at him, offending twice as much.
You do not love Maria? Longaville
Did never for her sake sonnet compile,
Nor never lay his wreathed arms apart
His loving bosom to keep down his heart?   135
I have been closely shrouded in this bush
And marked you both and both your man's-eyes push.
I heard your guilty rhymes, observed your fashion,
Saw sighs reek from you, noted well your passion.
"Why me," says one, "O Jove!" the other cries,   140
One, her hairs were gold; crystal the other's eyes.

(to Longaville)

You would for paradise break faith and troth;

(to Dumaine)

And Jove for your love would infringe an oath.
What will Berowne say when that he shall hear
Faith infringed which such zeal did swear?   145
How will he scorn, how will he spend his wit!

How will he triumph, leap and laugh at it!
For all the wealth that ever I did see,
I would not have him know so much by me.

BEROWNE *(comes forward)*

Now step I forth to whip hypocrisy.   150
Ah, my good liege, I pray thee pardon me.
Good heart, what grace do you have to reprove
These worms for loving, that are most in love?
Your eyes do make no coaches; in your tears
There is no certain princess that appears;   155
You'll not be perjured, 'tis a hateful thing;
Tush, none but minstrels like of sonneting!
But are you not ashamed? Nay, are you not,
All three of you, to be thus much overshot?
You found his flaw, the King your flaw did see;   160
But I a beam do find in each of three.
O, what a scene of foolery have I seen,
Of sighs, of groans, of sorrow, and of spleen!
O me, with what strict patience have I sat,
To see a king transformed to a gnat!   165
To see great Hercules whipping a gig,
And profound Solomon to tune a jig,
And Nestor play at push-pin with the boys,
And critic Timon laugh at idle toys.
Where lies your shame? O, tell me, good Dumaine.   170
And gentle Longaville, where lies thy pain?
And where my king's? All about the breast?
A candle, ho!

KING

Too bitter is your jest.
Are we betrayed thus by your scornful view?   175

58

BEROWNE

Not you to me, but I betrayed by you;
I that am honest, I that hold it sin
To break the vow I am so promised in —
I am betrayed by keeping company
With men like you, men of inconstancy.   180
When shall you see me write a thing in rhyme?
Or groan for Joan? Or spend a minute's time
In preening me? When shall you hear that I
Will praise a hand, a foot, a face, an eye,
A gait, a state, a brow, a breast, a waist,   185
A leg, a limb —

KING

Halt! Why walk away so fast?
A true man wouldn't need to gallop so?

BEROWNE

I post from love. Good lover, let me go.

Enter Jaquenetta with a letter and Costard

JAQUENETTA

God bless the king!   190

KING

What present have you there?

COSTARD

Some certain treason.

KING

What makes treason here?

COSTARD

No, it makes nothing, sir.

KING

If it mar nothing neither,   195
The treason and you go in peace away together.

JAQUENETTA

Please your grace let this letter be read.

Our person questions it; it was treason, he said.

KING

Berowne, read it over.

(Berowne reads the letter)

Who gave it to it?   200

JAQUENETTA

Costard.

KING

Where did you find it?

COSTARD

From Dun Adramadio, Dun Adramadio.

Berowne tears the letter up

KING

Aha, what's wrong with you? Why do you tear it?

BEROWNE

A toy, my liege, a toy. Your grace needs not fear it.   205

LONGAVILLE

It did move him to passion and therefore let's hear it.

DUMAINE (*picks up the pieces)*

It is Berowne's writing and here is his name.

BEROWNE *(to Costard)*

Ah, you whoreson peckerhead, you were born to do me shame.

Guilty, my lord, guilty: I confess, I confess.

KING

What?   210

BEROWNE

That you three fools lacked this fool to make up the mess.

He, he, and you — and you, my liege — and I

Are turtle-doves in love and we deserve to die.

O, dismiss this audience and I shall tell you more.

DUMAINE

Now the number is even.   215

BEROWNE

True, true, we are four.

Will these eyesores be gone?

KING

Hence, fools, away!

COSTARD

Walk aside the true folk and let the traitors stay.

Exit Costard and Jaquenetta

BEROWNE

Sweet lords, sweet lovers, O, let us embrace!   220

As true we are as flesh and blood can be,

The sea will ebb and flow, heaven show his face;

Young blood doth not obey an old decree.

We cannot change the cause why we are born;

Therefore of all hands must we be forsworn.   225

KING

What, did these torn lines show some love of thine?

BEROWNE

"Did they?" you ask! Who sees not heavenly Rosaline

And, like a man of rude, savage design,

At the first conquest of the gorgeous east,

Bows not his slavish head, and, strucken blind,   230

Kisses the base ground with obedient breast?

What unblinking eagle-sighted eye

Dares look upon the heaven of her brow

That is not blinded by her majesty?

KING

What zeal, what fury hath inspired thee now?   235

My love, her mistress, is a gracious moon;

She, an attending star, scarcely seems bright.

BEROWNE

    My eyes are then no eyes, nor I Berowne.
    O, but for my love, day would turn to night!
    Of all complexions the most elegant   240
    Do meet as at a fair in her fair cheek,
    Where several virtues make one dignity,
    Where nothing wants, that want itself doth seek.
    Lend me the flourish of all gentle tongues —
    Fie, painted rhetoric! O, she needs it not.   245
    To things for sale a seller's praise belongs:
    She passes praise; then praise too short doth blot.
    A withered hermit, five-score winters worn,
    Might shake off fifty, looking in her eye.
    Beauty doth polish age as if new born,   250
    And gives the crutch the cradle's infancy.
    O, 'tis the sun that maketh all things shine.

KING

    By heaven, your love is black as ebony!

BEROWNE

    Is ebony like her? O word divine!
    A wife of such wood were felicity.   255
    O, who can give an oath? Where is a book?
    That I may swear beauty does beauty lack
    If that she learn not of her eye to look.
    No face is fairer than that which is black.

KING

    O paradox! Black is the shade of hell,   260
    The hue of dungeons and the school of night,
    And beauty's crest becomes the heavens well.

BEROWNE

    Devils soonest tempt, resembling angels of light.
    O, if in black my lady's brows be decked,

It mourns that painting and usurping hair   265
Should ravish doters with a false aspect;
And therefore is she born to make black fair.
Her favour turns the fashion of the days,
For native blood is used by artists now;
And therefore red, that would avoid dispraise,   270
Paints itself black, to imitate her brow.

DUMAINE

To look like her are chimney-sweepers black.

LONGAVILLE

And since her time are undertakers counted bright.

KING

And Ethiops of their burnt complexion crack.

DUMAINE

Dark needs no candles now, for dark is light.   275

BEROWNE

Your mistresses dare never come in rain,
For fear their colours should be washed away.

KING

'Twere good yours did; for, sir, to tell you plain,
I'll find a fairer face not washed today.

BEROWNE

I'll prove her fair, or talk till doomsday here.   280

KING

No devil will fright thee then so much as she.

DUMAINE

I never knew man hold vile stuff so dear.

LONGAVILLE *(shows his shoe)*

Look, here's your love, my foot and her face see.

BEROWNE

O, if the streets were paved with thine eyes,
Her feet were much too dainty for such tread.   285

63

DUMAINE

O, vile! Then, as she goes, that flower lies
The street should see as she walked overhead.

KING

But what of this? Are we not all in love?

BEROWNE

O, nothing so sure, and thereby all forsworn.

KING

Then leave this chat and, good Berowne, now prove   290
Our loving lawful and our faith not torn.

DUMAINE

Yes, indeed, there; some flattery for this evil.

LONGAVILLE

O, some authority how to proceed.
Some tricks, some logic how to cheat the devil.

DUMAINE

Some salve for perjury.   295

BEROWNE

O, it's more than need.
Have at you then, affection's men-at-arms.
Consider what you first did swear unto:
To fast, to study, and to see no woman —
Flat treason against our kingly state of youth.   300
Men, can you fast? Your stomachs are too young,
And abstinence engenders sickly woes.
O, we have made a vow to study, lords,
And in that vow we have forsworn our books;
For when would you, my liege, or you, or you,   305
In heavy contemplation have found out
Such fiery verses as the prompting eyes
Of Beauty's daughters have enriched you with?
Academics are just kept in the brain,

64

And therefore, finding dull practitioners,   310
Scarce show a harvest of their heavy toil;
But love, first learned in a lady's eyes,
Lives not alone walled up in the brain
But with the strength of all the elements
Rushes as swift as thought in every sense   315
And gives to every sense a double sense,
Above their functions and their offices.
It adds a precious seeing to the eye:
A lover's eyes will gaze an eagle blind.
A lover's ear will hear the lowest sound   320
When thieves creep through the house with silken foot.
Love's feeling is more soft and sensible
Than tender belly of the nightingale.
Love's tongue proves dainty Dionysus gross in taste,
For valour, is not Love a Hercules,   325
Still climbing trees in the dainty breeze?
Subtle as Sphinx, as sweet and musical
As bright Apollo's lute, strung with his hair.
And when Love speaks, the voice of all the gods
Make heaven drowsy with the harmony.   330
Never dares poet touch a pen to write
Until his ink were tempered with Love's sighs.
O, then his lines would ravish savage ears
And plant in tyrants mild humility.
From women's eyes this doctrine I derive: 335
For they sparkle like the Promethean fire;
They are the books, the arts, the academes,
That show, contain and nourish all the world;
Else nothing, none at all proves excellent.
Then fools you were these women to forswear,   340
Or, keeping what is sworn, you will prove fools.

For wisdom's sake, a word that all men love,
Or, for love's sake, a word that loves all men,
Or, for men's sake, the poets of these women,
Or women's sake, by whom we men are men,   345
Let us once lose our oaths to find ourselves,
Or else we lose ourselves to keep our oaths.
It is religion to be thus forsworn,
For charity itself fulfills the law,
And who can sever love from charity?   350

KING

Saint Cupid, then! And, soldiers, to the field!

BEROWNE

Advance your standards and upon them, lords!
Take arms, down with them! But be first advised
In conflict that you get the suns of them.

LONGAVILLE

Now to plain dealing. Lay these word-games by.   355
Shall we resolve to woo these girls of France?

KING

And win them too! Therefore let us devise
Some entertainment for them in their tents.

BEROWNE

First, from the park let us conduct them thither.
Then homeward every man attach the hand   360
Of his fair mistress. In the afternoon
We will with some strange pastime amuse them,
Such as the shortness of the time can shape;
For revels, dances, masques, and merry hours
Forerun fair Love, strewing her way with flowers.   365

KING

Away, away! No time shall be omitted
That will be time and may by us be fitted.

BEROWNE

Go on, go on!

Exit the King, Longaville, and Dumaine

Sowed metal reaped no corn:

And justice always whirls in equal measure.   370

Crude wenches may prove plagues to men forsworn;

If so, our deserts are no better treasure.

Exit

ACT 5 ◆ SCENE 1

Enter Holofernes, Nathaniel, and Dull

HOLOFERNES

Enough is as good as a feast.

NATHANIEL

I praise God for you, sir. Your reasons at dinner have been
sharp and sanctimonious, pleasant without obscenity, witty
without affection, audacious without impudency, learned
without opinion, and fresh without blasphemy. I did con-   5
verse the other day with a companion of the King's, who is
entitled, nominated, or called, Don Adriano de Armado.

HOLOFERNES

I know him as well as I know you. His humour is lofty, his
discourse childish, his tongue rapid, his eye ambitious, his
walk majestical, and his general behaviour vain, ridiculous,   10
and boastful. He is too picky, too spruce, too affected, too
odd, as it were, too proudly travelled, as I may say.

NATHANIEL

A most singular and choice epithet.

Nathaniel draws out his table-book

HOLOFERNES

He draws out the thread of his verbosity finer than the staple
of his argument. I abhor such fanatical lunatics, such unso-   15
ciable and point-device companions, such novices of penmanship, as to speak "dout" without "b," when he should say
"doubt," "det" when he should pronounce "debt": d, e, b, t, not
d, e, t. He calls a calf "cauf," half "hauf," neighbour he calls
"nebour," neigh abbreviated "ne." This is abhominable, which   20
he would call "abominable." It insinuates insanity into me.

69

Do you understand, master? To make frantic, lunatic.

NATHANIEL

God be praised, I understand good.

HOLOFERNES

"Good"? "Good" for "well"! Grammar a little cracked; 'twill
serve.   25

Enter Armado, Moth, and Costard

NATHANIEL

See who comes?

HOLOFERNES

I see and I am glad.

ARMADO

Hola!

HOLOFERNES

Why "hola," not "sirrah"?

ARMADO

Men of peace, well encountered.   30

HOLOFERNES

Most military sir, salutation.

MOTH *(to Costard)*

They have been at a great feast of languages and stolen the
scraps.

COSTARD *(to Moth)*

O, they have lived long on the spoils of others' words! I wonder why your master has not eaten you for a word? For you   35
are not so wise in the head as to choke my lord. Thou are
easier swallowed than your words.

MOTH

Peace! The fun begins.

ARMADO *(to Holofernes)*

Monsieur, are you the educator?

MOTH

Yes, yes! He teaches boys the hornbook. What is a, b, spelled   40
backward with the horn on his head?

HOLOFERNES

Ba, child, with a horn added.

MOTH

Ba, most silly sheep with a horn. You hear his learning.

HOLOFERNES

What, what, you consonant?

MOTH

The last of the five vowels, if you repeat them; or the fifth, if I. 45

HOLOFERNES

I will repeat them: a, e, i —

MOTH

The sheep. The other two concludes it: o, u.

ARMADO

Now, by the salt wave of the Mediterranean, a sweet touch,
a quick venue of wit! Snip-snap, quick and home! It arouses
my intellect. True wit!   50

MOTH

Offered by a child to an old man — which is old wit.

HOLOFERNES

What is the figure? What is the figure?

MOTH

Horns.

HOLOFERNES

You dispute like an infant. Go, whip your gig.

MOTH

Lend me your horn to make one and I will whip about your 55
infamy. A gig of a cuckold's horn!

COSTARD

If I had but one penny in the world, you should have it to buy

gingerbread. Hold, there is the very remuneration I had of
thy master, you halfpenny purse of wit, you scrap of discretion. O, if the heavens were so pleased that you were but my   60
bastard, what a joyful father wouldst thou make me! Go to,
you have it *ad dunghill,* at the fingers' ends, as they say.

HOLOFERNES

O, I smell false Latin: "dunghill" for *unguem.*

ARMADO

A man of the arts! We will rise above the barbarous. Do
you not educate youth at the school-house on the top of the   65
mountain?

HOLOFERNES

Or *mons,* the hill.

ARMADO

At your sweet pleasure, for the mountain.

HOLOFERNES

I do, without question.

ARMADO

Sir, it is the King's most sweet pleasure and affection to con-   70
gratulate the Princess at her pavilion in the posteriors of this
day, which the rude multitude call the "afternoon."

HOLOFERNES

The posterior of the day, most generous sir, is liable, appro-
priate and measurable for the afternoon. The word is well
matched, choice, sweet, and apt, I do assure you, sir, I do   75
assure.

ARMADO

Sir, the king is a noble gentleman, and my familiar, I do
assure you, very good friend. For what is private between
us, let it pass. I do ask that you remember your courtesy: I
demand that you wear your hat. And among other import-   80
ant and most serious designs, and of great import indeed

too — but let that pass. For I must tell you it will please the
king, by the world, sometime to lean upon my poor shoulder
and with his royal finger thus dally with my excrement, with
my mustachio. But, sweet heart, let that pass. By the world,   85
I recount no fable! Some certain special honours it pleases
his greatness to impart to Armado, a soldier, a man of travel,
that has seen the world. But let that pass. The very all of all
is — but, sweet heart, I do implore secrecy — that the King
would have me present the Princess — a sweet lady — with   90
some delightful performance, or show, or pageant, or skit,
or firework. Now, understanding that your holy friend and
your sweet self are good at such eruptions and sudden break-
ing-out of mirth, as it were, I have acquainted you withal, to
the end to crave your assistance.   95

HOLOFERNES

Sir, you shall present before her the Nine Worthies. Sir
Nathaniel, as concerning some entertainment of time, some
show in the posterior of this day, to be rendered by our assis-
tants, the King's command and this most chivalrous, illus-
trate, and learned gentleman, before the Princess — I say,   100
none so fit as to present the Nine Worthies.

NATHANIEL

Where will you find men worthy enough to present them?

HOLOFERNES

Joshua, yourself; this gallant gentleman, Judas Maccabaeus;
this bum, because of his great limb or joint, shall pass Pompey
the Great; the page, Hercules.   105

ARMADO

Pardon, sir, error! He is not quantity enough for that Worthy's thumb. He is not so big as the end of his club.

HOLOFERNES

Shall I have audience? He shall present Hercules in minority.

73

His enter and exit shall be strangling a snake; and I will have
an apology for that purpose. 110

MOTH

An excellent device! So, if any of the audience hiss, you may
cry 'Well done, Hercules! Now you crush the snake!' That is
the way to make an offence gracious, though few have the
grace to do it.

ARMADO

For the rest of the Worthies? 115

HOLOFERNES

I will play three myself.

MOTH

Thrice-worthy gentleman.

ARMADO

Shall I tell you a thing?

HOLOFERNES

We attend.

ARMADO

We will have, if this fail not, a skit. Follow. 120

HOLOFERNES

Go, goodman Dull! You have spoken no word all this while.

DULL

Nor understood none neither, sir.

HOLOFERNES

Go on! We will employ thee.

DULL

I'll make one in a dance, or so; or I will play on the drum to
the Worthies, and let them dance in the hay. 125

HOLOFERNES

Most Dull, honest Dull! To our sport, away!

Exit all

ACT 5 ◆ SCENE 2

Enter the Princess, Rosaline, Maria, and Katherine

PRINCESS

    Sweet hearts, we shall be rich before we depart,

    If these riches come plentifully in.

    We will all be bedecked with diamonds!

    Look what I have received from the good King.

ROSALINE

    Madame, came nothing else along with that?   5

PRINCESS

    Nothing but this? Yes, as much love in rhyme

    As would be crammed up in a sheet of paper

    Writ on both sides the leaf, margin and all,

    That he was forced to seal on Cupid's name.

ROSALINE

    That was the way to make his manhood wax,   10

    For he has been five thousand year a boy.

KATHERINE

    Yes, and send him to the gloomy gallows too.

ROSALINE

    You'll never be friends with him: he killed your sister.

KATHERINE

    He made her melancholy, sad and heavy;

    And so she died. Had she been light, like you,   15

    Of such a merry, nimble, stirring spirit,

    She might have been a grandma before she died.

    And so may you, for a light heart lives long.

ROSALINE

    What's your dark meaning, mouse, of this light word?

KATHERINE

    A light condition in a beauty dark.   20

ROSALINE

We need more light to find your meaning out.

KATHERINE

You'll mar the light by taking it in snuff;

Therefore I'll darkly end the argument.

ROSALINE

Look what you do, you do it still in the dark.

KATHERINE

So do not you, for you are a light wench. 25

ROSALINE

Indeed I weigh not you, and therefore light.

KATHERINE

You weigh me not? O, that's you care not for me!

ROSALINE

Great reason, for past care is still past cure.

PRINCESS

Well played both! A set of wit well played.

But, Rosaline, you have a favour too: 30

Who sent it? And what is it?

ROSALINE

I would you knew.

And if my face were but as fair as yours,

My favour were as great. Be witness this:

Nay, I have verses too, I thank Berowne; 35

The numbers true, and, were the numbering too,

I were the fairest goddess on the ground.

I am compared to twenty thousand fairs.

O, he hath drawn my picture in his letter!

PRINCESS

Anything like? 40

ROSALINE

Much in the letters, nothing in the praise.

PRINCESS

Beauteous as ink: a good conclusion.

KATHERINE

Fair as an ink blot in a copy-book.

ROSALINE

Beware pencils, ho! Let me not die your debtor,

My red-faced commoner, my hue is better.   45

O, that your face was not so full of nose!

PRINCESS

A pox of that jest and I beshrew all shrews.

But, Katherine, what was sent to you from fair Dumaine?

KATHERINE

Madam, this glove.

PRINCESS

Did he not send you twain?   50

KATHERINE

Yes, madam, and moreover

Some thousand verses of a faithful lover,

A huge translation of hypocrisy,

Vilely compiled, profound simplicity.

MARIA

This and these pearls Longaville sent to me.   55

His letter is too long by half a mile.

PRINCESS

I think no less. Dost thou not wish in heart

The chain were longer and the letter short?

MARIA

Ay, or I would these hands might never part.

PRINCESS

We are wise girls to mock our lovers so.   60

ROSALINE

They are worse fools to purchase mocking so.

That same Berowne I'll torture before I go.
O how I ensnared him within a week!
How I will make him fawn, and beg, and seek,
And wait the season, and observe the times,   65
And spend his prodigal wits in bootless rhymes,
And shape his service all to my requests,
And make him proud to make me proud that jests!
So like-for-like would I oversway his state,
That he should be my fool, and I his fate.   70

PRINCESS
None are so surely caught, when they are catched,
As wit turned fool. Folly, in wisdom hatched,
Has wisdom's warrant and the help of school
And wit's own grace to grace a learned fool.

ROSALINE
The blood of youth burns not with such excess   75
As when a scholar turns to lustful stress.

MARIA
Folly in fools bears not so strong a note
As foolery in the wise when wit does dote,
Since all the power thereof it does apply
To prove, by wit, worth in simplicity.   80

Enter Boyet

PRINCESS
Here comes Boyet, and his big grinning face.

BOYET
O, I am stabbed with laughter! Where's her grace?

PRINCESS
Your news, Boyet?

BOYET
Prepare, madam, prepare!
Ladies, get ready! Encounters mounted are   85

Against your peace. Love does approach disguised,
Armed in arguments: you'll be surprised.
Muster your wits, stand in your own defence,
Or hide your heads like cowards and fly hence.

PRINCESS

Saint Joan against Saint Cupid! What are they   90
That charge their breath against us? Say, scout, say.

BOYET

Under the cool shade of a sycamore
I thought to close my eyes for half an hour,
When, lo, to interrupt my purposed rest,
Toward that shade I might behold addressed   95
The King and his companions. Warily
I hid inside a neighbour's thicket by
And overheard what you shall overhear:
That, by and by, disguised they will be here.
Their herald is a pretty, knavish lord   100
That well by heart has learned his sweet love-word.
Action and accent did they teach him there:
"Thus must you speak and thus your body bear."
And ever and anon they made a doubt
Presence majestical would put him out;   105
"For," said the King, "an angel shalt thou see;
Yet fear not you, but speak audaciously."
The boy replied, "An angel is not evil;
I should have feared her had she been a devil."
With that all laughed and clapped him on the shoulder,   110
Making the bold wag by their praises bolder.
One rubbed his elbow thus, and grinned, and swore
A better speech was never spoke before.
Another with his finger and his thumb
Cried, "Come all, we will do't, come what will come!"   115

The third he capered and cried, "All goes well!"
The fourth turned on the toe, and down he fell.
With that they all did tumble on the ground,
With such a zealous laughter, so profound,
That in this ridiculous spleen appears,   120
To check their folly, passion's solemn tears.

PRINCESS

But what, but what, come they to visit us?

BOYET

They do, they do, and are apparelled thus:
Like Muscovites, or Russians, as I guess.
Their purpose is to talk, to court and dance,   125
And every one his love-suit will advance
Unto his particular mistress, which they'll know
By favours several which they did bestow.

PRINCESS

And will they so? The lovesick shall be tasked;
For, ladies, we will every one be masked,   130
And not one man of them shall have the grace,
Despite of suit, to see a lady's face.
Here, Rosaline, this favour thou shalt wear,
And then the King will court thee for his dear.
You take thou this, my sweet, and give me thine,   135
So shall Berowne take me for Rosaline.
And change your favours too; so shall your loves
Woo contrary, deceived by these fair gloves.

ROSALINE

Come on, then, wear the favours most in sight.

KATHERINE

But in this changing what is your intent?   140

PRINCESS

The effect of my intent is to cross theirs.

They do it but in mocking merriment,
And mock for mock is only my intent.
Their wooing speeches they acknowledge shall
To loves mistook, and so be mocked withal   145
Upon the next occasion that we meet,
With visages displayed to talk and greet.

ROSALINE

But shall we dance, if they desire us to it?

PRINCESS

No, to the death, we will not move a foot;
Nor to their penned speech render we no grace,   150
But while it's spoke each turn away her face.

BOYET

Why, that contempt will kill the speaker's heart
And quite divorce his memory from his part.

PRINCESS

Therefore I do it, and I make no doubt
The rest will e'er come in, if he be out.   155
There's no such sport as sport by sport o'erthrown,
To make theirs ours and ours none but our own.
So shall we stay, mocking intended game,
And they, well mocked, depart away with shame.

Sound trumpet

BOYET

The trumpet sounds. Be masked. The villains come.   160

Enter Blackamoors with music, Moth with a speech,
and the King, Berowne, Longaville, and Dumaine disguised

MOTH

All hail the richest beauties on the earth!

BEROWNE

Beauties no richer than rich golden thread.

MOTH

A holy parcel of the fairest dames.
(the ladies turn their backs to him)
That ever turned their — backs — to mortal views.

BEROWNE

Their eyes, villain, *their eyes.*   165

MOTH

That ever turned their eyes to mortal views!
Out —

BOYET

True! Out indeed!

MOTH

Out of your favours, heavenly spirits, promise
Not to behold —   170

BEROWNE

Once to behold, rogue!

MOTH

Once to behold with your sun-beamed eyes —
With your sun-beamed eyes —

BOYET

They will not answer to that epithet.
You were best call it "daughter-beamèd eyes."   175

MOTH

They do not mark me and that brings me out.

BEROWNE

Is this your performance? Be gone, you rogue!

Exit Moth

ROSALINE

What would these strangers? Know their minds, Boyet.
If they do speak our language, 'tis our will
That some plain man recount their purposes   180
Know what they would.

BOYET

What would you with the Princess?

BEROWNE

Nothing but peace and gentle visitation.

ROSALINE

What would they, say they?

BOYET

Nothing but peace and gentle visitation.   185

ROSALINE

Why, that they have, and bid them so be gone.

BOYET

She says you have it and you may be gone.

KING

Say to her, we have measured many miles

To tread a measure with you on the grass.

BOYET

They say that they have measured many a mile   190

To tread a measure with you on this grass.

ROSALINE

It is not so. Ask them how many inches

Is in one mile? If they have measured many,

The measure then of one is easily told.

BOYET

If to come hither you have measured miles,   195

And many miles, the Princess bids you tell:

How many inches amounts to one mile?

BEROWNE

Tell her we measure them by weary steps.

BOYET

She hears herself.

ROSALINE

How many weary steps,   200

Of many weary miles you have overgone,
Are numbered in the travel of one mile?

BEROWNE

We number nothing that we spend for you.
Our duty is so rich, so infinite,
That we may do it still without account.   205
O, show me then the sunshine of your face,
That we like savages may worship it.

ROSALINE

My face is but a moon and clouded too.

KING

Blessed are clouds, to do as such clouds do.
Promise, bright moon, and these your stars, to shine —   210
Those clouds removed — upon our watery eyne.

ROSALINE

O vain stranger! Beg a greater matter:
You now request but moonshine in the water.

KING

Then, in our measure promise but one dance.
You bid me beg: is this my only chance?   215

ROSALINE

Play music then! Nay, you must do it soon.
(music plays)
Not yet? No dance! Thus change I like the moon.

KING

Will you not dance? Why are you so estranged?

ROSALINE

You took the moon at full, but now she's changed.

KING

Yet still she is the moon, and I the man.   220
The music plays, permit some motion to it.

ROSALINE

Our ears permit it.

KING

But your legs should do it.

ROSALINE

Since you are strangers and come here by chance,

We'll not be nice. Take hands. We will not dance.   225

KING

Why take my hand then?

ROSALINE

Only to part friends.

Curtsy, sweet hearts, and so the measure ends.

Music stops

KING

More measure of this measure! This was nice.

ROSALINE

We can afford no more at such a price.   230

KING

Price you yourselves. What buys your company?

ROSALINE

Your absence only.

KING

That can never be.

ROSALINE

Then cannot we be bought. And so adieu —

Twice to your visor and half once to you!   235

KING

If you deny to dance, let's hold more chat.

ROSALINE

In private then.

KING

I am best pleased with that.

The King and Rosaline converse apart

BEROWNE

Fair-handed mistress, one sweet word with thee.

PRINCESS

Honey, and milk, and sugar: there is three. 240

BEROWNE

Nay then, two three, and if you grow so nice,

Cherubim, toys and trifles. Well run, dice!

There's half-a-dozen sweets.

PRINCESS

Seventh sweet, adieu.

Since you can cheat, I'll play no more with you. 245

BEROWNE

One word in secret.

PRINCESS

Let it not be sweet.

BEROWNE

You stir my gall.

PRINCESS

Gall? Bitter.

BEROWNE

Therefore meet. 250

The Princess and Berowne converse apart

DUMAINE

Will you permit with me to change a word?

MARIA

Name it.

DUMAINE

Fair lady —

MARIA

Say you so? Fair lord!

Take you that for your "fair lady." 255

DUMAINE

Please it you,

As much in private and I'll bid adieu.

Maria and Dumaine converse apart

KATHERINE

What, was your visor made without a tongue?

LONGAVILLE

I know the reason, lady, why you ask.

KATHERINE

O, for your reason! Quickly, sir, I long.   260

LONGAVILLE

You have a double tongue within your mask

And would afford my speechless visor half.

KATHERINE

You have a silver tongue — is not that dull?

LONGAVILLE

Ay, dull, fair lady.

KATHERINE

No, fair lord is dull.   265

LONGAVILLE

Let's half the word.

KATHERINE

No, I'll not be your half.

Take calf and wean it, it may prove an ox.

LONGAVILLE

Look how you butt yourself in these sharp mocks.

Will you give horns, chaste lady? Do not so.   270

KATHERINE

Then die a calf before your horns do grow.

LONGAVILLE

One word in private with you ere I die.

KATHERINE

Bleat softly then; the butcher hears you cry.

Katherine and Longaville converse apart

BOYET *(aside)*

The tongues of mocking ladies are as keen

As is the razor's edge invisible,   275

Cutting a smaller hair than may be seen;

Above the sense of sense, so sensible

Seeming their conference. Their conceits have wings

Faster than arrows, bullets, wind, thought, swifter things.

ROSALINE

Not one word more, my maids; break off, break off.   280

BEROWNE

By heaven, all dry-beaten with pure scoff!

KING

Farewell, mad ladies. You have simple wits.

Exit the King, Lords, and Blackamoors

PRINCESS

Twenty adieus, my frozen Muscovites.

Are these the breed of wits so wondered at?

BOYET

Candles they are, with your sweet breaths puffed out.   285

ROSALINE

Well-liking wits they have; gross, gross, fat, fat.

PRINCESS

O poverty in wit, his humour's out!

Will they not, think you, hang themselves tonight?

Or ever but in visors show their faces?

This pert Berowne was out of countenance quite.   290

ROSALINE

They were all in lamentable cases.

The King was weeping-ripe for a good word.

PRINCESS

Berowne did swear himself out of all suit.

MARIA

Dumaine was at my service, and his sword.

'No point,' said I: my servant straight was mute.   295

KATHERINE

Lord Longaville said I came o'er his heart;

And know you what he called me?

PRINCESS

Ill perhaps?

KATHERINE

Yes, in good faith.

PRINCESS

Go, sickness as you are!   300

ROSALINE

Well, better wits have worn plain dunces-caps.

But will you hear? The King is my love sworn.

PRINCESS

And quick Berowne hath plighted faith to me.

KATHERINE

And Longaville was for my service born.

MARIA

Dumaine is mine as sure as bark on tree.   305

BOYET

Madam, and pretty mistresses, give ear:

Immediately they will again be here

In their own shapes, for it can never be

They will digest this harsh indignity.

PRINCESS

Will they return?   310

BOYET

They will, they will, God knows;

89

And leap for joy, though they are lame with blows:
Therefore change favours and, when they repair,
Blow like sweet roses in this summer air.

PRINCESS

Why "blow"? Why "blow"? Speak to be understood. 315

BOYET

Fair ladies masked are roses in their bud;
Unmasked, their blushing sweet complexion shown,
Are angels moving clouds, or roses blown.

PRINCESS

Enough perplexity! What shall we do
If they return in their own shapes to woo? 320

ROSALINE

Good madam, if by me you'll be advised
Let's mock them still, as well known as disguised.
Let us complain to them what fools were here,
Disguised like Muscovites, in shapeless gear;
And wonder what they were and to what end 325
Their shallow shows and prologue vilely penned,
And their rough carriage so ridiculous,
Should be presented at our tent to us.

BOYET

Ladies, withdraw. The lovers are at hand.

PRINCESS

Whip to our tents, as does run o'er land. 330

Exit the Princess, Rosaline, Katherine, and Maria
Enter the King, Berowne, Longaville, and Dumaine, as themselves

KING

Fair sir, God save you. Where's the Princess?

BOYET

Gone to her tent. Please it your majesty
Command me any service to her?

KING

That she would give me audience for one word.

BOYET

I will; and so will she, I know, my lord. 335

Exit

BEROWNE

This courtier pecks up wit as magpies gold
And utters it again when God hath told.
He is wit's dealer and resells his wares
At wakes and parties, meetings, markets, fairs;
And we that sell by gross, the Lord does know, 340
Have not the grace to charm wit with such show.
This weasel pins the ladies on his sleeve.
Had he been Adam, he had tempted Eve.
He can lisp and charm too. Why, this is he
That kissed away his hand in courtesy. 345
This is the ape of form, Monsieur the Nice,
That when he plays at tables chides the dice
In honourable terms. Nay, he can sing
A song most sweetly, and in his writing
Poesy pours forth. The ladies call him sweet. 350
The stairs, as he treads on them, kiss his feet.
This is the flower that smiles on everyone,
To show his teeth as white as whale's bone;
And scaling dukes that will not die in debt
Pay him the due of "honey-tongued Boyet." 355

KING

A blister on his sweet tongue, with my heart,
That put Armado's page out of his part!

Enter the Princess, Rosaline, Maria, and Katherine, with Boyet

BEROWNE

See where it comes! Behaviour, what were you

Till this man showed you? And what now are you?

KING

All hail, sweet madam, and fair time of day.   360

PRINCESS

"Fair" in "all hail" is foul, as I conceive.

KING

Construe my speeches better, if you may.

PRINCESS

Then wish me better; I will give you leave.

KING

We came to visit you and purpose now

To lead you to our court. Permit us then.   365

PRINCESS

This field shall hold me, and so hold your vow.

Nor God nor I delight in lying men.

KING

Rebuke me not for that which you provoke.

The virtue of your eye must break my oath.

PRINCESS

You nickname virtue: "vice" you should have spoke;   370

For virtue's office never breaks men's oaths.

Now, by my maiden honour, yet as pure

As the unsullied lily, I protest,

A world of torments though I should endure,

I would not yield to be your house's guest,   375

So much I hate a breaking cause to be

Of heavenly oaths, vowed with integrity.

KING

O, you have lived in desolation here,

Unseen, unvisited, much to our shame.

PRINCESS

Not so, my lord. It is not so, I swear.   380

We have had pastimes here and pleasant game:
A mess of Russians left us but of late.

KING

How, madam? Russians?

PRINCESS

Ay, in truth, my lord.
Trim lovers, full of courtship and of state.   385

ROSALINE

Madam, speak true! It is not so, my lord.
My lady, to the manner of the days,
In courtesy gives undeserving praise.
We four indeed confronted were with four
In Russian habit. Here they stayed an hour,   390
And talked apace; and in that hour, my lord,
They did not bless us with one happy word.
I dare not call them fools; but this I think,
When they are thirsty, fools would die to drink.

BEROWNE

This jest is dry to me. My gentle sweet,   395
Your wits makes wise things foolish. When we greet,
With eyes best seeing, heaven's fiery eye,
By light we lose light. Your capacity
Is of that nature that to your huge store
Wise things seem foolish and rich things but poor.   400

ROSALINE

This proves you wise and rich, for in my eye —

BEROWNE

I am a fool, and full of poverty.

ROSALINE

But that you take what does to you belong,
It were a fault to snatch words from my tongue.

BEROWNE

O, I am yours, and all that I possess.   405

ROSALINE

All the fool mine?

BEROWNE

I cannot give you less.

ROSALINE

Which of the visors was it that you wore?

BEROWNE

Where, when, what visor? Why demand you this?

ROSALINE

There, then, that visor: that superfluous case   410
That hid the worse and showed the better face.

KING

We are descried. They'll mock us now downright.

DUMAINE

Let us confess and turn it to a jest.

PRINCESS

Amazed, my lord? Why looks your highness sad?

ROSALINE

Help! Hold his brows! He'll swoon. Why look you pale?   415
Sea-sick, I think, coming from Muscovy!

BEROWNE

Thus pour the stars down plagues for perjury.
Can any brazen face hold longer out?
Here stand I lady; dart thy skill at me.
Bruise me with scorn, confound me with a pout,   420
Thrust your sharp wit quite through my ignorance,
Cut me to pieces with your keen conceit,
And I will wish you never more to dance,
Nor never more in Russian costume wait.
O, never will I trust to speeches penned,   425

Nor to the motion of a schoolboy's tongue,
Nor never come in visor to my friend,
Nor woo in rhyme like a blind minstrel's song.
Velvet-soft phrases, silken terms precise,
Three-piled hyperboles, spruce affectation,   430
Figures pedantical: these summer flies
Have blown me full of maggot ostentation.
I do forswear them, and I here protest,
By this white glove — how fair the hand, God knows! —
Henceforth my wooing mind shall be expressed   435
In rustic yeas and honest copper noes.
And, to begin, lady, so God help me, law!
My love to you is sound, *sans* crack or flaw.

ROSALINE

Sans "sans," I pray you.

BEROWNE

Yet I have a trick   440
Of the old rage. Bear with me, I am sick;
I'll leave it by degrees. Soft, let us see:
Write, "Lord have mercy on us" on those three.
They are infected, in their hearts it lies;
They have the plague and caught it of your eyes.   445
These lords are visited: you are not free,
For the Lord's tokens on you do I see.

PRINCESS

No, they are free that gave these tokens to us.

BEROWNE

Our states are forfeit. Seek not to undo us.

ROSALINE

It is not so; for how can this be true,   450
That you stand forfeit, being those that woo?

BEROWNE

Peace! for I will not have to do with you.

ROSALINE

Nor shall not if I do as I intend.

BEROWNE *(to the other lords)*

Speak for yourselves. My tongue is at an end.

KING

Teach us, sweet madam, for our rude transgression   455
Some fair excuse.

PRINCESS

The fairest is confession.

Were you not here but even now, disguised?

KING

Madam, I was.

PRINCESS

And were you well advised?   460

KING

I was, fair madam.

PRINCESS

When you then were here,

What did you whisper in your lady's ear?

KING

That more than all the world I did respect her.

PRINCESS

When she shall challenge this, you will reject her.   465

KING

Upon mine honour, no.

PRINCESS

Peace, peace, forbear!

Your oath once broke, you force not to forswear.

KING

Despise me when I break this oath of mine.

PRINCESS

    I will; and therefore keep it. Rosaline, 470

    What did the Russian whisper in your ear?

ROSALINE

    Madam, he swore that he did hold me dear

    As precious eyesight and did value me

    Above this world; adding thereto, moreover,

    That he would wed me, or else die my lover. 475

PRINCESS

    God give thee joy of him. The noble lord

    Most honourably doth uphold his word.

KING

    What mean you, madam? By my life, my troth,

    I never swore this lady such an oath.

ROSALINE

    By heaven you did! And to confirm it plain, 480

    You gave me this; but take it, sir, again.

KING

    My faith and this the Princess I did give.

    I knew her by this jewel on her sleeve.

PRINCESS

    Pardon me, sir, this jewel did she wear,

    And Lord Berowne, I thank him, is my dear. 485

    What! Will you have me or your pearl again?

BEROWNE

    Neither of either, I remit both twain.

    I see the trick on it. Here was a conceit,

    Knowing beforehand of our merry cheat,

    To dash it like a Christmas comedy. 490

    Some idiot, some yes-man, some slight zany,

    Some gossiper, some false-knight, some Dick

    That smiles his cheek in years and knows the trick

To make my lady laugh when she's disposed,
Told our intents before; which, once disclosed,   495
The ladies did change favours and then we,
Following the signs, wooed but the sign of she.
Now, about our lying to add more terror,
We are again caught up in will and error.
This is what this is. *(to Boyet)* And was not you   500
Forestall our sport, to make us thus untrue?
Do not you know my lady's foot by size,
And laugh upon the apple of her eye?
And stand between her back, sir, and the fire,
Holding a platter, jesting merrily?   505
You put our page out — Go, you are allowed;
Die when you will, a dress shall be your shroud.
You leer upon me, do you? There's an eye
Wounds like a pointless sword.

BOYET

    Full merrily   510
Have these brave insults, this hot mouth been run.

BEROWNE

    Lo, he is rising straight. Peace! I have done.

Enter Costard

    Welcome, pure wit! You're leaving a fair fray.

COSTARD

    O lord, sir, they would know
Whether the three Worthies shall come in or no.   515

BEROWNE

    What, are there but three?

COSTARD

    No, sir, but it is very fine,
For every one presents three.

BEROWNE

And three times thrice is nine.

COSTARD

Not so, sir — under correction, sir — I hope it is not so. You 520
cannot beg us, sir, I can assure you, sir; we know what we
know. I hope, sir, three times thrice, sir —

BEROWNE

Is not nine?

COSTARD

Under correction, sir, we know to what it doth amount.

BEROWNE

By Jove, I always took three threes for nine. 525

COSTARD

O Lord, sir, it were pity you should get your living by count-
ing, sir.

BEROWNE

How much is it?

COSTARD

O Lord, sir, the parties themselves, the actors, sir, will show
to what it doth amount. For mine own part, I am, as they 530
say, but to perfect one man in one poor man — Pompion the
Great, sir.

BEROWNE

Art thou one of the Worthies?

COSTARD

It pleased them to think me worthy of Pompey the Great. For
my own part, I know not the degree of the Worthy, but I am 535
to stand for him.

BEROWNE

Go bid them prepare.

COSTARD

We will turn it finely off, sir; we will take some care.

Exit

KING

Berowne, they will shame us. Let them not approach.

BEROWNE

We are shame-proof, my lord; and 'tis some policy   540

To have one show worse than the King's and his company.

KING

I say they shall not come.

PRINCESS

No, my good lord, let me overrule you now.

That sport best pleases that does least know how —

Where love strives for content and the contents   545

Fall in the love of that which it presents;

There form so rude makes most form in mirth,

When great things labouring perish in their birth.

BEROWNE

A right description of our sport, my lord.

Enter Armado

ARMADO

Anointed, I implore so much expense of your royal sweet 550
breath as will utter a brace of words.

Armado and the King talk apart

PRINCESS

Does this man serve God?

BEROWNE

Why ask you?

PRINCESS

He speaks not like a man of God his making.

ARMADO

That's all one, my fair, sweet, honey monarch; for, I protest, 555
the schoolmaster is exceeding fantastical; too, too vain; too,
too vain; but we will put it, as they say, to the chance of war.

(Armado gives the King a paper)

I wish you the peace of mind, most royal couple.

Exit

KING

Here is likely to be a good presentation of the Nine Worthies.
He presents Hector of Troy; the bum, Pompey the Great; the   560
parish curate, Alexander; Armado's page, Hercules; the pedant, Judas Maccabaeus.

(reading)

And if these four Worthies in their first show thrive,
These four will change habits and present the other five.

BEROWNE

There is five in the first show.   565

KING

You are deceived; 'tis not so.

BEROWNE

The pedant, the braggart, the priest, the fool, and the boy.
Travel wherever, and the whole world again
Cannot prick out five such men, take each one in's vein.

KING

The ship has sailed — let's hope it does not rain.   570

Enter Costard as Pompey

COSTARD

I Pompey am —

BEROWNE

You lie, you are not he.

COSTARD

I Pompey am —

BOYET

With leopard's head on knee.

BEROWNE

Well said, old mocker. I must needs be friends with thee.   575

101

COSTARD

I Pompey am, Pompey surnamed the Big.

DUMAINE

The "Great."

COSTARD

It is "Great," sir; *Pompey surnamed the Great,*
That oft in field, with sword and shield, did make my foe to sweat;
And travelling along this coast, I here am come by chance,   580
And lay my arms before the legs of this sweet lass of France.
If your ladyship would say, "Thanks Pompey," I had done.

PRINCESS

Great thanks, great Pompey.

COSTARD

'Tis not so much worth, but I hope I was perfect. I made a
little fault in "Great."   585

BEROWNE

My hat to a halfpenny, Pompey proves the best of the Worthies.

Enter Nathaniel for Alexander

NATHANIEL

When in the world I lived, I was the world's commander;
By east, west, north, and south, I spread my conquering might;
My armour doth declare that I am Alexander.

BOYET

Your nose says no, you are not; for it stands too right.   590

BEROWNE

Your nose smells "no" in this, most tender-smelling knight.

PRINCESS

The conqueror is dismayed. Proceed, good Alexander.

NATHANIEL

When in the world I lived, I was the world's commander —

BOYET

Most true, 'tis right: you were so, Alexander.

BEROWNE

Pompey the Great —   595

COSTARD

Your servant, and Costard.

BEROWNE

Take away the conqueror; take away Alexander.

COSTARD *(to Nathaniel)*

O sir, you have overthrown Alexander the conqueror. You
will be etched out of history for this. Your lion, that holds
his axe sitting on a throne, will be given to a bum. He will   600
be the ninth Worthy. A conqueror, and afeard to speak? Run
away for shame, Alexander. *(Nathaniel retires)* There, if it shall
please you, a foolish mild man; an honest man, look you, and
soon dashed. He is a marvellous good neighbour, faith, and
a very good bowler; but for Alexander, alas, you see how it is   605
— a little over-parted. But there are Worthies a-coming will
speak their mind in some other sort.

PRINCESS

Stand aside, good Pompey.

Enter Holofernes as Judas and Moth as Hercules

HOLOFERNES

Great Hercules is presented by this imp,
Whose club killed Cerberus, that three-headed canus,   610
And when he was a babe, a child, a shrimp,
Thus did he strangle serpents in his manus.
But since he seemeth in minority,
Ergo *I come with this apology.*
Keep some state in thy exit, and vanish.   615

Moth retires

Judas I am —

DUMAINE

A Judas!

103

HOLOFERNES

Not Iscariot, sir.

Judas I am, and dubbed Maccabaeus.

DUMAINE

Judas Maccabaeus clipped is plain Judas.   620

BEROWNE

A kissing traitor. How, art thou proved Judas?

HOLOFERNES

Judas I am —

DUMAINE

The more shame for you, Judas.

HOLOFERNES

What mean you, sir?

BOYET

To make Judas hang himself.   625

HOLOFERNES

Begin, sir: you are my elder.

BEROWNE

Well followed: Judas was hanged on an elder.

HOLOFERNES

I will not be put out of character.

BEROWNE

Because you have no face.

HOLOFERNES

What is this?   630

BOYET

A maidenhead.

DUMAINE

The head of a hair-pin.

BEROWNE

A death's face in a frame.

LONGAVILLE

The face of an old Roman coin, scarce seen.

BOYET

The handle of Caesar's dagger. 635

DUMAINE

The carved-bone face on a flask.

BEROWNE

Saint George's half-cheek in a brooch.

DUMAINE

Ay, and in a brooch of lead.

BEROWNE

Ay, and worn in the cap of a doctor — remember you will die.

And now forward, for we have put you in character. 640

HOLOFERNES

You have put me out of character.

BEROWNE

False! We have given you faces.

HOLOFERNES

But you have outfaced them all.

BEROWNE

If you were a liar, we would do so.

BOYET

Therefore, as he is an ass, let him go. 645

And so adieu, sweet Jude. Nay, why do you stay?

DUMAINE

For the latter end of his name.

BEROWNE

For the ass to the Jude? Give it him: Jud-ass, away!

HOLOFERNES

This is not generous, not gentle, not humble.

BOYET

A light for Monsieur Judas! It grows dark; he may stumble. 650

Holofernes retires

PRINCESS

Alas, poor Maccabaeus, how he has been baited!

Enter Armado as Hector

BEROWNE

Hide your head, Achilles! Here comes Hector in arms.

DUMAINE

Though my mocks come home by me, I will now be merry.

KING

Hector was but a Trojan in respect of this.

BOYET

But is this Hector?   655

KING

I think Hector was not so well-built.

LONGAVILLE

His leg is too big for Hector's.

DUMAINE

More calf, certain.

BOYET

No, he is best endowed in the small.

BEROWNE

This cannot be Hector.   660

DUMAINE

He's a god or a painter, for he makes faces.

ARMADO

The formidable Mars, of lances the almighty,

Gave Hector a gift —

DUMAINE

A flower.

BEROWNE

A field.   665

LONGAVILLE

A garden.

DUMAINE

No, a bush.

ARMADO

Peace!

The formidable Mars, of lances the almighty,
Gave Hector a gift, heir of ill-fated Troy;   670
A man so breathed that certain he would fight, yea,
From morn till night, out of his pavilion.
I am that flower —

DUMAINE

That pine!

LONGAVILLE

That dandelion!   675

ARMADO

Sweet Lord Longaville, rein your tongue.

LONGAVILLE

I must rather give it the rein, for it runs against Hector.

DUMAINE

Ay, and Hector's a greyhound.

ARMADO

The sweet war-man is dead and rotten. Sweet birds beat not
the bones of the buried. When we breathed, he was a man. 680
But I will forward with my speech. Sweet royalty, bestow on
me the sense of hearing.

PRINCESS

Speak, brave Hector; we are much delighted.

ARMADO

I do adore your sweet grace's slipper.

BOYET

Loves her by the foot.   685

DUMAINE

He may not by the yard.

ARMADO

This Hector far surmounted Hannibal;

The party is gone —

COSTARD

Fellow Hector, she is gone! She is two months on her way.

ARMADO

What do you mean?   690

COSTARD

Faith, unless you play the honest Trojan, the poor wench is cast away: she's quick, the child brags in her belly already. It's yours.

ARMADO

Do you defy me among the court? You shall die!

COSTARD

Then shall Hector be whipped for Jaquenetta that is quick by   695 him and hanged for Pompey that is dead by him.

DUMAINE

Most rare Pompey!

BOYET

Renowned Pompey!

BEROWNE

Greater than "Great." Great, great, great Pompey! Pompey the huge!   700

DUMAINE

Hector trembles.

BEROWNE

Pompey is moved. More strife, more strife! Stir them on, stir them on!

DUMAINE

Hector will challenge him.

BEROWNE

Yes, if he have no more man's blood in his belly than will sup   705
a flea.

ARMADO

By the north pole, I do challenge you.

COSTARD

I will not fight with a stick like a northern man. I'll slash, I'll
do it by the sword. I pray you, let me borrow my arms again.

DUMAINE

Room for the incensed Worthies.   710

COSTARD

I'll do it in my shirt.

DUMAINE

Most resolute Pompey!

MOTH

Master, let me take you a buttonhole lower. Do you not see,
Pompey is uncasing for the combat. What mean you? You
will lose your reputation.   715

ARMADO

Gentlemen and soldiers, pardon me. I will not combat in my
shirt.

DUMAINE

You may not deny it. Pompey has made the challenge.

ARMADO

Sweet bloods, I both may and will.

BEROWNE

What reason have you for it?   720

ARMADO

The naked truth of it is, I have no shirt. I go woolward for
penance.

MOTH

True, and it was enjoined him in Rome for want of linen.

Since when, I'll be sworn he wore none but a dishcloth of
Jaquenetta's, and that he wears next his heart for a favour.   725

Enter a Messenger, Monsieur Marcadé

MARCADÉ

God save you, madam.

PRINCESS

Welcome, Marcadé,

But that you interrupt our merriment.

MARCADÉ

I am sorry, madam, for the news I bring

Is heavy in my tongue. The King, your father —   730

PRINCESS

Dead, for my life!

MARCADÉ

Even so; my tale is told.

BEROWNE

Worthies, away! The scene begins to cloud.

ARMADO

For mine own part, I breathe free breath. I have seen the day
of wrong through the little hole of discretion and I will right   735
myself like a soldier.

Exit Worthies

KING

How now your majesty?

PRINCESS

Boyet, prepare. I will away tonight.

KING

Madam, not so. I do beg of you, stay.

PRINCESS

Prepare, I say. I thank you, gracious lords,   740

For all your fair endeavours, and entreat,

Out of a new-sad soul that you permit

In your rich wisdom to excuse or hide
The merry sport of our contentious quips,
If over-boldly we have borne ourselves   745
In the converse of breath. Your gentleness
Was guilty of it. Farewell worthy lord!
A heavy heart bears not a nimble tongue.
Excuse me so, coming too short of thanks
For my great suit so easily obtained.   750

KING

In times like these, good Time himself does lift
The mist of human strife so Man can see
And often at the very end decides
That which long process could not arbitrate.
And though the royal daughter's mourning brow   755
Denies the smiling courtesy of Love
His chance to wed her with a holy vow,
Yet, since love's argument has long been here,
Let not the cloud of sorrow shadow it.
To dutifully bewail a friend who's lost   760
Is not by much so wholesome-profitable
As to rejoice at friends but newly found.

PRINCESS

I understand you not. My griefs are double.

BEROWNE

Honest plain words best pierce the ear of grief;
And by these fair words understand the King.   765
For your fair sakes have we neglected time,
Played foul play with our oaths. Your beauty, ladies,
Has much deformed us, fashioning our passions
Even to the opposed end of our intents;
And what in us has seemed ridiculous —   770
As love is full of unbefitting strains,

All wanton as a child, skipping and vain,
Formed by the eye and therefore, like the eye,
Full of strange shapes, of habits and of forms,
Varying in subjects as the eye it rolls   775
To every varied object in his glance;
If multicoloured apparels of love
Put on by us, do in your heavenly eyes,
Misdirect our good oaths and gravities,
Those heavenly eyes that look into these faults,   780
Suggested that we make. Therefore, ladies,
Our love being yours, the error that love makes
Is likewise yours. We to ourselves prove false
By being once false, forever to be true
To those that make us both — fair ladies, you.   785
And even that falsehood, in itself a sin,
Thus purifies itself and turns to grace.

PRINCESS

We have received your letters full of love,
Your favours, the ambassadors of love,
And in our maiden council rated them   790
At courtship, pleasant jest and courtesy,
As stuffing and as lining to the time.
But more devout than this in our respects
Have we not been; and therefore met your loves
In their own fashion, like a merriment.   795

DUMAINE

Our letters, madam, showed much more than jest.

LONGAVILLE

So did our looks.

ROSALINE

We did not quote them so.

KING

    Now, at the latest minute of the hour,

    Grant us your loves.   800

PRINCESS

    A time, methinks, too short

    To make an everlasting promise in.

    No, no, my lord, your grace is perjured much,

    Full of dear guiltiness; and therefore this:

    If for my love — though there is no such cause —   805

    You will do aught, this shall you do for me:

    Your oath I will not trust, but go with speed

    To some forlorn and naked hermitage,

    Remote from all the pleasures of the world,

    There stay until the twelve celestial signs   810

    Have took their annual ring around the sun.

    If this austere insociable life

    Change not your offer made in heat of blood;

    If frosts and fasts, hard lodging and thin weeds,

    Nip not the gaudy blossoms of your love,   815

    But that it bear this trial and last love;

    Then at the expiration of the year,

    Come challenge me, challenge me by these words,

    And, by this virgin palm now kissing yours,

    I will be yours. I, till that instance, shut   820

    My woeful self up in a mourning house,

    Raining the tears of lamentation

    For the remembrance of my father's death.

    If this you do deny, let our hands part,

    Neither entitled in the other's heart.   825

KING

    If this, or more than this, I would deny,

    To flatter up these powers of mine with rest,

113

The sudden hand of death close up mine eye!
Hence, hermit then — my heart is in your breast.

The King and The Princess converse apart

DUMAINE

But what to me, my love? But what to me?   830
A wife?

KATHERINE

A beard, fair health and honesty;
With three-fold love, I wish you all these three.

DUMAINE

O, shall I say "I thank you, gentle wife"?

KATHERINE

Not so, my lord. A twelvemonth and a day   835
I'll mark no words that smooth-faced wooers say.
Come when the King does to my lady come;
Then, if I have much love, I'll give you some.

DUMAINE

I'll serve you true and faithfully till then.

KATHERINE

Yet swear not, lest you be forsworn again.   840

Katherine and Dumaine converse apart

LONGAVILLE

What says Maria?

MARIA

At the twelvemonth's end
I'll change my black gown for a faithful friend.

LONGAVILLE

I'll stay with patience, but the time is long.

MARIA

O just like you; few taller are so young.   845

Maria and Longaville converse apart

114

BEROWNE

Studies, my lady? Mistress, look on me.
Behold the window of my heart, mine eye,
What humble suit attends thy answer there.
Impose some service on me for your love.

ROSALINE

Oft have I heard of you, my Lord Berowne,   850
Before I saw you. And the world's large tongue
Proclaims you for a man supplied with mocks,
Full of comparisons and wounding jests,
Which you on all estates will execute
That lie within the mercy of your wit.   855
To weed this sickness from your fruitful brain
And there within to win me, if you please —
Without the which I am not to be won —
You shall this twelvemonth term from day to day
Visit the speechless sick and still converse   860
With groaning wretches; and your task shall be
With all the fierce endeavour of your wit
To turn the convalescent pains to smiles.

BEROWNE

To move wild laughter in the throat of death?
It cannot be, it is impossible: 865
Mirth cannot move a soul in agony.

ROSALINE

Why, that's the way to choke a mocking spirit,
Whose influence is begot of that loose grace
Which shallow laughing hearers give to fools.
A jest's prosperity lies in the ear   870
Of him that hears it, never in the tongue
Of him that makes it. Then, if sickly ears,
Deafed with the clamours of their own dear groans,

Will hear your idle scorns, continue then,
And I will have you and that fault withal;   875
But, if they will not, throw away that spirit,
And I shall find you empty of that fault,
Right joyful of your reformation.

BEROWNE

A twelvemonth? Well, befall what will befall,
I'll jest a twelvemonth in an hospital.   880

PRINCESS *(to the King)*

Ay, sweet my lord, and so I take my leave.

KING

No, madam, we will bring you on your way.

BEROWNE

Our wooing doth not end like an old play:
Jack hath not Jill. These ladies' courtesy
Might well have made our sport a comedy.   885

KING

Come, sir, it wants a twelvemonth and a day,
And then 'twill end.

BEROWNE

That's too long for a play.

Enter Armado

ARMADO

Sweet majesty, allow me —

PRINCESS

Was not that Hector?   890

DUMAINE

The worthy knight of Troy.

ARMADO

I will kiss your royal finger and take leave. I am a votary; I
have vowed to Jaquenetta to hold the plough for her sweet
love three year. But, most esteemed greatness, will you hear

the dialogue that the two learned men have compiled, in 895
praise of the owl and the cuckoo? It should have followed in
the end of our show.

KING

Call them forth quickly; we will do so.

ARMADO

Holla! Approach.

Enter Holofernes, Nathaniel, Costard,
Dull, Jaquenetta, Moth

This side is Hiems, winter; this Ver, the spring: the one main- 900
tained by the owl, th'other by the cuckoo. Ver, begin.

THE SONG

VER

When daisies pied and violets blue
And lady-smocks all silver-white
And cuckoo-buds of yellow hue
Do paint the meadows with delight,   905
The cuckoo then on every tree
Mocks married men; for thus sings he: "Cuckoo!
Cuckoo, cuckoo!" O, word of fear,
Unpleasing to a married ear.

When shepherds pipe on oaten straws   910
And merry larks are ploughmen's clocks,
When turtles tread and rooks and daws,
And maidens bleach their summer smocks,
The cuckoo then, on every tree,
Mocks married men; for thus sings he: "Cuckoo!   915
Cuckoo, cuckoo!" O, word of fear,
Unpleasing to a married ear.

HIEMS

When icicles hang by the wall
And Dick the shepherd blows his nail
And Tom bears logs into the hail   920
And milk comes frozen home in pail,
When blood is nipped and ways be foul,
Then nightly sings the staring owl:
"Tu-whit, Tu-whoo!"
A merry note,   925
While greasy Joan doth stir the pot.

When all aloud the wind doth blow
And coughing drowns the parson's saw
And birds sit brooding in the snow
And Marian's nose looks red and raw,   930
When roasted crabs hiss in the bowl,
Then nightly sings the staring owl:
"Tu-whit, Tu-whoo!"
A merry note,
While greasy Joan doth stir the pot.   935

ARMADO

The words of Rhetoric are harsh after the songs of Apollo. You
that way, we this way.

Exit

FINIS

MOTH'S SONG

When Colinet was making love (bis),
With his velvet fur hat (bis),
And his beautiful jacket,
Who never did, who never said:
Colinet, my friend,   5
And his beautiful jacket,
True Lord, he's so pretty

Alas! Guillaume,
Over the green, over the grey, over the yellow,
Alas! Guillaume, would you let yourself die over it!   10

Colinet goes for a walk (bis)
With his mistress at Ducler (bis),
To give himself a career
Who never did, who never said:
Colinet, my friend,   15
To give himself rear,
Isn't he so pretty!

Alas! Guillaume,
Over the green, over the grey, over the yellow,
Alas! Guillaume, would you let yourself die over it!   20

When Colinet comes back from the fields (bis)
He wants someone to rub his cock (bis),
In order for him to enter,

Who never did, who never said:
Colinet, my friend,   25
In order for him to enter,
Within the little hole?

Alas! Guillaume,
Over the green, over the grey, over the yellow,
Alas! Guillaume, would you let yourself die over it!   30

When Colinet wants to get closer (bis),
His wife does nothing but to scold (bis),
Telling him that his male organ
Who never did, who never said:
Colinet, my friend,   35
Telling him that his male organ
Is too soft and too small:

Alas! Guillaume,
Over the green, over the grey, over the yellow,
Alas! Guillaume, would you let yourself die over it!   40

The Hell, it'll be sold (bis)
And cut right off my butt (bis),
Despite my wife,
Who never did, who never said:
Colinet, my friend,   45
Despite my wife,
Who says it's too small:

Alas! Guillaume,
Over the green, over the grey, over the yellow,
Alas! Guillaume, would you let yourself die over it!   50

Let's sell ewes, let's sell sheep (bis),
Let's sell whatever we have,
Let's not sell this limb,
Who never did, who never said:
Colinet, my friend,   55
Let's not sell this limb,
Which makes peace in the bed:

Alas! Guillaume,
Over the green, over the grey, over the yellow,
Alas! Guillaume, would you let yourself die over it!   60